JOURNEY WITH PAUL

A Simplified Survey of the
Pauline Books

JOURNEY WITH PAUL

A Simplified Survey of the Pauline Books

SAMUEL LEE

FOUNDATION UNIVERSITY PRESS

JOURNEY WITH PAUL

A Simplified Survey of the Pauline Books

SAMUEL LEE

Published by Foundation University Press

Verrijn Stuartweg 31, Diemen 1112 AW, The Netherlands

www.foundationuniversity.com

This book or parts thereof may not be reproduced in any form, stored in a retrieval system or transmitted in any form by any means-electronic, mechanical, photocopy, recording or otherwise- without prior written permission of the publisher, except as provided by the European Copyright Law and United States of America Copyright Law.

978-90-79516-02-5

Copyright © 2009 by Foundation University Press

CONTENTS

Introduction		1
Lesson 1	The Apostle Paul	3
Lesson 2	Romans: The Gospel of Paul Part I	13
Lesson 3	Romans: The Gospel of Paul Part II	25
Lesson 4	I Corinthians: Orderly Worship & Christian Life	33
Lesson 5	II Corinthians: Suffering for Christ	45
Lesson 6	Galatians: The Truth of the Gospel	51
Lesson 7	Ephesians Part I: The Book of God's Call	57
Lesson 8	Ephesians Part II: Spiritual Warfare	67
Lesson 9	Philippians: The Book of Joy	75
Lesson 10	Colossians: Paul's Defense	83
Lesson 11	I & II Thessalonians: Paul on Lord's Coming	91

Lesson 12	I & II Timothy: Pastoral Epistles Part I	97
Lesson 13	Titus: Pastoral Epistles Part II	107
Lesson 14	Philemon: A Free Slave	113
Lesson 15	Last Journey	119
About the Author		123
About JCF Ministries		125
Dr. Samuel Lee's Websites		127
Invite Dr. Samuel Lee		129
Other Books by Samuel Lee		131
Audio Sermons		133

Introduction

Journey with Paul is a simplified theology of one of the great pillars of Christianity as an organized religion. The Apostle Paul's teachings have affected the Church in such a manner that even today we are benefiting from them. The ideas of the Apostle Paul were revolutionary at that time; if it had been left up to the ordinary Christians during the time of Jesus, Christianity would have contained in Israel and some parts of the Middle East, and attainable for the Jews only. The Apostle Paul, however, opened the doors of the gospel for both Jews and Gentiles, and therefore to the entire known world of that time.

The Apostle Paul's teachings offer us the hope of resurrection, the assurance of salvation for the Gentiles, and co-heir of the Father's inheritance as fellow children of Abraham. The Apostle Paul was also an authoritative and disciplined teacher. He raised up many sons and daughters in the faith, such as Timothy, and passed on his mandate to them for further advancement of the Gospel of Christ. Paul was also a zealot for the Gospel and boldly opposed false teachers and their doctrines. He has been often tortured, beaten, stoned, and imprisoned, but none of these consequences stopped him from preaching the Gospel. Christianity grows day by day in various parts of the world, and the mixture of Christianity with the "Hollywood" style of faith, commercializing its beliefs, abusing the name of the Holy Spirit, merchandizing the church, over-rich church leaders, discrimination, racism and segregation in the church today; these are only a few things which I believe Paul would radically address if he would have lived today. However, this is our task. Even today, we need men and women like Paul to rise up and deal with these issues. The Apostle Paul was a reformer; we too need to be reformers, and once we have reformed those issues needing reformation, then we have to start reforming the things we just reformed, and so keep on reforming, keep on watching, keep on being critical.

Finally, there is an important point to mention: often many Christian leaders, even some theologians, mistakenly interpret the Bible through the teachings of the Apostle Paul. However, Christ and His teachings are the foundation of all books in the Bible and, in particular, the New Testament. Therefore as you read this book, or while reading the Pauline books in the Bible, you should measure them based on the words of Jesus Christ, the foundation of our Faith. Paul is not the cornerstone of Christendom, but Jesus Christ is!

This book is a systematical exploration of the Pauline Books in the *Holy Bible*, which can be easily used in Bible study groups, cell groups, churches and seminaries. Every lesson consists of verses to memorize and questions to answer individually or for discussion in a group setting. Let us walk in the steps of the Apostle Paul and start the journey.

LESSON 1

THE APOSTLE PAUL

Lesson 1

THE APOSTLE PAUL

INTRODUCTION

Before entering this tremendous spiritual journey throughout the books of the New Testament, and in particular the books of the Apostle Paul, we need to know about the life of the apostle and his teachings in general; who was this man and what did he contribute to the foundations of our faith so that still today both believers and non-believers admire his life and teachings? Where was he when Jesus started His ministry? This lesson lays a foundation that facilitates a more effective understanding of the books of Paul.

TODAY'S JOURNEY

Who is Paul?

Paul was born in a Jewish family in Tarsus, a city in today's southeast Turkey. During the first century however, this city was a part of the Roman Empire, and that is why Paul considered himself a citizen of Rome. The date of his birth is unknown, but we assume that he was younger than Jesus.

The Roman Empire was considered the most advanced, modern, and liberal nation in the world. A comparison can be made between the Roman Empire and the contemporary United States of America. As it is today, many people do everything they can to become an American citizen, and many people in those days wanted to become a citizen of the Roman Empire.

Paul grew up and was educated in Jerusalem; he was trained to be a Pharisee. He was intellectual and could speak three different languages — Latin, Greek and Hebrew. The Jews knew him as Saul, which was his Jewish name, but right after his conversion he received a new name, 'Paul'. Paul literally means "little." Paul was not among the twelve disciples who were chosen by Jesus in His earthly life. In fact, we know little of the apostle's childhood and his life during the three years of Jesus' ministry. Some believe that Paul even witnessed the crucifixion of Jesus Christ in Jerusalem.

The first time we read about Paul is in the Book of Acts. It was during the persecution and stoning of Stephen (Acts 7:54–60): *"At this they covered their ears and, yelling at the top of their voices, they all rushed at him [Stephen], dragged him out of the city and began to stone him. Meanwhile, the witnesses laid their clothes at the feet of a young man named Saul"* (Acts 7:57–58). These passages are the first place in the Bible where Saul's name is mentioned. Saul, a religious leader in training to become a Pharisee, began persecuting Christians the very day of Stephen's death. *"Saul began to destroy the church. Going from house to house, he dragged off men and women and put them in prison"* (Acts 8:3).

The day Stephen died, Saul, a persecutor of Christians, did not know the Father's plans of using him to teach the Gospel to the world. In Acts Chapter 9, we read about the radical conversion of Saul: *"Meanwhile, Saul was still breathing out murderous threats against the Lord's disciples. He went to the high priest and asked him for letters to the synagogues in Damascus, so that if he found any there who belonged to the Way, whether men or women, he might take them as prisoners to Jerusalem"* (Acts 9:1–2).

On his way to Damascus, the Lord Jesus Christ appeared to him supernaturally and changed his life radically. From that day on he became a preacher of the Gospel.

The Benjaminite

Paul is one of the fathers of Christianity; he is the author of a large part of the New Testament, and his writings have been influencing the Church for the past 2000 years. The early Church believed that Paul was even prophetically mentioned even in the Old Testament, similar to Jesus.

The most famous statement in the Old Testament which refers to Paul is found in Genesis 49:27. This is the passage where Jacob, at the end of his life, was blessing his sons. The words he spoke to his son Benjamin are considered the statements which refer to Paul: *"Benjamin is a ravenous wolf; in the morning he devours the prey, in the evening he divides the plunder"* (Genesis 49:27).

This is much like a description of Paul's character. He was from the tribe of Benjamin and was like a wolf; devouring and plundering the church of Jesus Christ in the time of early Christianity. But when God called and changed Paul during the dark times of persecutions and martyrdom in Church history, he became a preacher of the Gospel. He distributed the most important food; spiritual food, which are his letters to those he once tried to persecute.

His Ministry

Paul's ministry was filled with challenges and adventures. He did his best to educate those whom he evangelized. His ministry reached a vast region encompassing Arabia, Spain, and other parts of the Balkan area. It's interesting to note that in some churches, like in the Syrian Antioch, he was teaching believers who had run away from Palestine because of his terrible persecution.

In total Paul had four journeys:

- First, with Barnabas and Mark (46–48 AD) (Acts 13–14)
  Book: Galatians
- Second, with Silas (49–52 AD) (Acts 14:39–18:22)
  Books: 1 & 2 Thessalonians
- Third, (53–57 AD) (Acts 18:23–21:16)
  Books: 1 & 2 Corinthians, Romans
- Fourth, (59–62 AD) (Acts 27–28:16)
  Books: Ephesians, Philippians, Colossians, Philemon, 1 & 2 Timothy

Paul was first imprisoned in Jerusalem for about two years, but he appealed in Rome's Imperial Court and therefore had to be transferred from Jerusalem to Rome. This was his fourth missionary journey. There, Nero had him killed. According to the early church writings we know, he was beheaded in Rome through the command of the Roman Caesar.

His Letters

Paul wrote the following books or letters:

- Romans
- 1 & 2 Corinthians
- Galatians
- Ephesians
- Philippians
- Colossians
- 1 & 2 Thessalonians
- 1 & 2 Timothy

- Titus
- Philemon

The books of Timothy and Titus are known as the Pastoral and Church Handbooks, because in these books Paul deals with church administration. The other books were named after the cities where he either established a church or fellowships of believers. These then, are the letters he wrote instructing them in the ways of life and faith in Christ Jesus.

His Character

Paul was an extraordinary man. He never compromised with the hypocrisy of religion in any form. He was highly educated, and therefore he was an intellectual person. He can be compared to modern day sociologists or anthropologists, for he knew a lot about different cultures and customs. The following is a summary of his character based on his faith:

- *He was not ashamed of the Gospel of Christ* **(Romans 1:16)**

  He was very zealous and very loyal, but at the same time, hot tempered for the sake of righteousness.

- *He was Jew with a Jew, gentile with gentile* **(1 Corinthians 9:20)**

  This characteristic allowed him to be the apostle to the gentiles while God also used him strongly among Jewish people.

- *He was also a normal man with inner battles* **(Romans 7:14–25)**

  This characteristic kept him from being proud and made him humble before both men and God.

The most important of Paul's ministries was the preaching of the good news to the gentiles, uniting Jews and non-Jews through the Gospel of Christ and redemption, which comes through the death and resurrection of Jesus. That is why his mission was not easy; the Jews persecuted him while at the same time he had difficult times with the gentiles. For example, the Jews circumcised their sons and abstained from eating certain foods. According to Paul's teachings, Christians do not need these laws (referring to eating or abstaining from unclean things) in order to be a good believer; rather, Christians need a total change of heart and to accept Christ as Savior. Hypocrisy regarding religious laws like these made him furious and therefore, we see in the Bible that he argues with Peter or with other apostles. In those days he also had to fight unrighteousness in the Church, especially against the teachings of the false apostles. He did not consider himself the greatest apostle; in fact, he felt he was the least among them. He was also quite timid and humble when he was with people, but in his teachings he was a strong man.

His Teachings

The writings of Paul were inspired by the Holy Spirit. These teachings were, and still are, innovative and reform-oriented, especially in Paul's time. As mentioned earlier, Paul often brought the Gospel to the gentiles (those who are not Jews). The Romans, Greeks, Arabs, were all gentiles with different cultures and religions. Bringing the gospel to them was not easy, not only because of the difference in cultural beliefs, but also because Christianity first began among the Jews and Jesus was a Jew. Therefore, many early Jewish Christians had problems accepting the non-Jewish Christians. Many Jewish Christians thought that Christianity was only meant for them. The teachings of Paul are summarized in the following: Spiritual Doctrines & Church Management Doctrines.

Spiritual Doctrines

- **Law:** man is not justified by observing the law, but by grace which comes through faith in Jesus Christ
- **Salvation:** is for every one who believes in Christ Jesus regardless of nationality, gender or race
- **Resurrection:** he strongly believed in the resurrection of Jesus Christ and said that if Christ had not risen from the dead the message he preached was futile and useless. There are many other topics on Paul's teachings, but some of the most important ones are the three above-mentioned points.

Church Management Doctrines

- **Order:** church as a fellowship had to be organized and orderly
- **Leadership:** genuine leaders serve, they don't rule
- **Social/Family matters:** he emphasized having a healthy husband & wife relationship, parents and children, church leaders and members.

Questions

- Describe in your own words the character of Paul.
- What are the main teachings of Paul?
- Can you explain why the teachings of the Apostle Paul are essential in Christianity, even in our modern day world?

Memorize

Romans 1:16

"I am not ashamed of the Gospel, because it is the power of God for salvation of every one who believes: first for Jews, then for gentiles."

LESSON 2

ROMANS:
THE GOSPEL OF PAUL PART I

CHAPTERS 1–11

Lesson 2

ROMANS: *THE GOSPEL OF PAUL PART I*

CHAPTERS 1–11

INTRODUCTION TO ROMANS

The book of Romans is considered one of the most important books written by the Apostle Paul in the New Testament. The book of Romans is written to the believers in Rome in the form of a letter.

Many people consider Romans the "seed" of the whole Bible, in which the basic message of the gospel is revealed to us through the Holy Spirit. Some call it the Gospel of Paul. One might say that Romans is the summary of the entire Holy Bible, whereby the will and plan of God is revealed to every human being. In Romans, the Apostle Paul deals with the issues of sin and its effects on human beings; he explains that we all have sinned and need a way out in order to be saved and forgiven by God. Therefore, God sent His Son Jesus Christ so that by believing in Him we are forgiven and are declared righteous. Paul wrote this book on his third missionary journey while he was on his way to bring the contributions of the churches in Macedonia and Achaia to the poverty-stricken believers of Jerusalem. Majority of these believers were gentiles with a minority group composed of Jewish Christians. The book of Romans may be divided in two major sections:

- God's Righteousness to all men through faith in Christ and His Grace (Romans 1–11)

    Paul deals with the wickedness of all man- the sin and the solution, that comes through Jesus Christ both for the Israelites and Gentiles.

- How to live as a Christian towards God, Church and Society (Romans 12–16)

    Paul emphasizes on Christian living, especially in those times of heavy persecutions and massacres of the Christians.

TODAY'S JOURNEY

The Wickedness of Men!

The book of Romans starts with a great and horrible statement: *"the wrath of God against mankind."* In Romans 1:18–32, Paul explains the root of a depraved world. Reading these passages clearly explains the current situation of our world and the reasons why our world is stated in such terrible conditions.

The Apostle Paul speaks of three important characteristics of a fallen man or society, which have been influencing the condition of our world from the beginning until today:

1. Sinful desires
2. Shameful lusts
3. Depraved minds

Sinful Desires

"The wrath of God is being revealed from heaven against all the godlessness and wickedness of men who suppress the truth by their wickedness" (Romans 1:18).

The Apostle says that human beings have no excuse for ignoring the existence of God and yet they do it. Because, according to him, since the creation of the world, God's signs, both natural and spiritual, were given to us so that by looking at them we may know that God exists. *"For since the creation of the world God's invisible qualities — His eternal power and divine nature-have been clearly seen being understood from what has been made, so that men are without excuse"* (Romans 1:20).

In other words, through looking at the Creation- the stars, the moon, the trees, the mountains, the birds etc... we are granted the opportunity to sense that there must be someone more intelligent than us; someone who is above all and everything; someone who is called GOD who has created all these things, including ourselves. But sadly, even though many people know God and sense His existence, they ignore the very fact of His being. These kinds of people abound today, and because of this ignorance, God will give them over to the sinful desires of their hearts. If we ever want our societies to be free from sexual immorality, violence, and other wicked acts, society must reconcile with God. Mothers and fathers need to come back to their senses, governments need to repent and come to the Creator of the heavens and earth and be reconciled to Him.

Shameful Lusts

Sinful desires bring forth shameful lusts: *"Because of this (sinful acts), God gave them over to shameful lusts..."* (Romans 1:26). What are then these shameful lusts? Paul explains in the extension of verse 26 the following: *"Even their women exchanged natural relations for unnatural ones. In the same way, the men also abandoned natural relations with women and were inflamed with lust for one another. Men committed indecent acts with other men, and received in themselves the due penalty for their perversion"* (Romans 1:26–27).

Homosexuality is not an issue that exists only today. This question goes back to centuries ago. For instance, the Greeks openly practiced homosexuality in the classical age; the same is true for the Roman Empire. Even in the church there are disputes about homosexuality. It is clear in the Bible that God does not tolerate homosexual lifestyles. Nevertheless, there are people, as well as Christians, who have such feelings. We should deal with them in God's love and through love allow them to see the truth, rather than continually condemning them. Much of the Christian world is afraid of homosexuals, and harbors the problem of an ongoing homophobia. We should not hate homosexuals, or isolate them, but through Christ's love help them in their battles. The Apostle Paul is addressing a deprived lifestyle; meaning that there are homosexuals as well as heterosexuals who live indecent lives, making others victims of their lust and desires.

I once met a homosexual Christian who explained that he loves Jesus with all his heart and knows what Jesus demands from him. Therefore, even though he has these feelings inside him, he chooses to live a life of solitude without practicing homosexuality. He was very honest in confessing his weakness, and yet chose a decent life. In contradiction to this man, there are also Christians with wives and children who have adulterous relationships and secretly living indecent lifestyles. The problem is uncontrollable lust and desires that cause people to do indecent things.

Depraved Minds

Shameful lusts are just the beginning of something worse: *depraved minds*. What is a depraved mind as Paul uses the term? It means to do what ought not to be done:

"They have become filled with every kind of wickedness, evil, greed and depravity. They are full of envy, murder, strife, deceit, and malice. They are gossipers, slanderers, God-haters, insolent, arrogant and boastful; they invent ways of doing evil; they disobey their parents; they are senseless, heartless, and ruthless.

Although they know God's righteous decree that those who do such things deserve death, they not only continue to do these very things but also approve of those who practice them" (Romans 1:28–32).

Do these acts remind you of something? Yes, it's a picture of our current world. In fact it seems as if the Apostle Paul is living in our time and perhaps even in our city! A 'depraved mind' is the highest form of illness and rebellion in a society. The tragedy is also in the verse in which Paul states: *"Although they know God's righteous decree that those who do such things deserve death, they not only continue to do these very things but also **approve of those who practice them**."* Focus here on the word *"approve"!* This is similar to what we call *"approving and tolerating under the umbrella of democracy."*

In our current world, people try to approve many things in the name of democracy! Today, under the shadow of democracy's approvals, a man lives with a man, a woman with a woman and in some countries can even adopt a child. All of these are approved by depraved minds, those who have ignored the existence of God as the Creator and worshiped the created things instead. This is the result of a human race that loves money more than God.

God's Judgment upon Men

"But because of your stubbornness and unrepentant heart, you are storing up wrath against yourself for the day of God's wrath, when his righteous judgment will be revealed. God will give to each person according to what he has done" (Romans 2:5–6).

Paul is warning the Romans that the Lord will judge the world, and everyone will receive what he/she deserves. Every child-abuser, woman beater, and killer will be judged before God, and His wrath will strike them, unless something radical changes in their lives before they die! God will bring every act to judgment, whether hidden or not! Many evildoers conduct their evil deeds in secret, thinking that no one will know about it; right now there are thousands of criminals walking around freely without any conviction of sin. God will surely judge them, for sooner or later they will appear before Him to face their final verdict.

God's Judgment upon His Own People

The book of Romans, however, does not only warn the nonbelievers, but also both the Jewish and Christian believers. The Church in Rome was a mixture of Jewish believers who were converted to Christianity and the native Romans, the gentiles who believed in Jesus Christ.

The Christian Jews were called the Messianic Jews. These Jews were Christians yet they held to their traditions and laws according to Moses, and by doing that they condemned and judged the gentiles who did not know the law, but because of their faith in Jesus they became Christians.

"Now, if you call yourself a Jew; if you rely on the law and brag about your relationship to God; if you know his will and approve of what is superior because you are instructed by the law; if you are convinced that you are guide for the blind, a light for those who are in the dark, an instructor for the foolish, a teacher of the infants, because you have the law the embodiment of knowledge and truth-you, then, who teach others, do you not teach yourself? You who preach against stealing, do you steal? You who say that people should not commit adultery, do you commit adultery? You who abhor idols, do you rob temples? You who brag about the law, do you dishonor God by breaking the law? As it is written: "God's name is blasphemed among the gentiles because of you" ... A man is not a Jew if he is only one outwardly, nor is circumcision

merely outward and physical. No, a man is a Jew if he is one inwardly, and circumcision is circumcision of the heart, by the Spirit, not by written code. Such man's praise is not from men, but from God" (Romans 2:17–29).

Even though the Apostle Paul was addressing the Messianic Jews, I believe that his words are upright and valid for some of us Christians today; some people have forgotten the actual matter of the Gospel and they believe in things of the outward; *such as holding the Sabbath only on Saturdays, or obeying the law in the Old Testament as hard as they can.* We also have people who brag about their gifts in the spirit and judge others who are not like them. For example, they are proud of their gift of tongues and so on, but they forget that being a Christian is not about outward appearances, but it is about the inner being. God knows and searches the motives of every person's heart. Christians who brag about their spirituality are empty people, people without a proper understanding who speak spiritually and yet do not live a life worthy of Christ. Just as the Apostle Paul addressed them: *"God's name is blasphemed among the gentiles because of you"* (Romans 2:24).

Today many people do not want to hear anything about Christianity because of the wrongdoings of some Christians. Some people want to believe in Christ without them being labeled as "Christian." This is sad and heartbreaking for God. Someone said once to me: "I want to believe in Jesus Christ, but I do not want to be called a Christian!" If Christians could be more loving and caring without religious and judgmental disputes, thousands of homosexuals would have the chance to come to Christ and be transformed and renewed before they realize that they are changed. It is the love of Christ through us and "the Word Became Flesh in us" that can set people free; when this happens there will be no place for argument because "He who the Son has set free is free indeed."

God's Righteousness

"There is no one righteous, not even one; there is no one who understands, no one who seeks God. All have turned away, they have together become worthless..." (Romans 3:10–11). The Apostle Paul also mentioned in Romans that the law was there to show us the standards of life, and by breaking the law or disobeying it we were declared sinners and unrighteous. Therefore, through observing the law, we can become righteous. Through the law we become more conscious about sin (Romans 3:19–20). However, another type of righteousness mentioned above is revealed to us through Jesus Christ. This righteousness comes through faith in Christ to all who believe in His sacrifice and redemption on the cross. Jesus became the sacrifice, and through His blood grace was released to those who believe in Him, and therefore sins are forgiven:

"Blessed are they whose transgressions are forgiven, whose sins are covered. Blessed is the man whose sin the lord will never count against him" (Romans 4:7–8).

Discrimination Issues

The Apostle Paul explicitly mentioned that this salvation and forgiveness are not only for the Jews but also for the gentiles. Today, there are many churches that even discriminate against other Christians from different backgrounds, cultures and races. This is against the love of God and His grace. In the kingdom of God there is no discrimination, there are no favorite nations, persons, or things. We are all one family, the family of Christ: *"Therefore, there is now no condemnation for those who are in Christ Jesus, because through Jesus Christ the law of the Spirit of life set me free from the law of sin and death"* (Romans 8:1–2).

Advantages of God's Righteousness

Eventually, Paul emphasizes the privileges of being a Christian and living by the righteousness of God.

- **We become Children of God**

  "For you did not receive a spirit that makes you slave again to fear, but received the Spirit of sonship. And by him we cry Abba Father... Now we are children, then we are heirs-heirs of God and co-heirs with Christ, if indeed we share in his sufferings in order that we may also share in His glory" (Romans 8:15–17).

- **Favor**

  "And we know that in all things God works for the good of those who love him, who have been called according to his purpose" (Romans 8:28).

- **More than Conquerors**

  "No, in all these we are more than conquerors through him who loved us" (Romans 8:37).

- **Shame-free**

  "Anyone who trusts in him will never be put to shame" (Romans 10:11).

Of course, there are many advantages and blessings that come through faith in Jesus Christ. However, the righteousness of God in us makes us His children, which gives us many rights and favors. The righteousness of God helps us in times of trouble because of His favor upon us — even if we are going through the darkest times of our lives, He can use these situations for our good. In other words, we have victory in many ways. This favor not only makes us winners, but it also renders us shame-free. God will always glorify Himself in us, in any and every situation, as long as we believe and trust in Him.

Questions

1. Explain the three characteristics of the fallen man.
2. What does it mean when we talk about the righteousness of God?
3. What are the conditions in order to gain this righteousness?

Memorize

Romans 10:11

"Anyone who trusts in him will never be put to shame."

LESSON 3

ROMANS: *THE GOSPEL OF PAUL PART II*

CHAPTERS 12–16

Lesson 3

ROMANS: *THE GOSPEL OF PAUL PART II*

CHAPTERS 12–16

The second part of the book of Romans, as I mentioned in the previous letter, is considered the way of Christian living or life. From Romans 12 until the end, Paul focuses on three important matters:

- How to be a Christian and what our attitude should be towards others, both believers and non-believers
- The position of Christians towards the government
- How to deal with false teachers

TODAY'S JOURNEY

Christian Living

Christian living means living as a true Christian in all aspects of life. It is easy to say, but how we actually live as Christians is a complicated issue! After Jesus Christ, the Apostle Paul is once again one of the pioneers on this subject. Keep in mind that the

Christian faith was born out of the Jewish tradition; the Mosaic Law had not become international and yet had to reach others besides the Jews. The Gospel of Christ that was preached by Paul was the gospel of grace and mercy through faith in Him. This opened the Gospel to the gentiles. However, one issue was how a non-Jewish Christian could live according to the new faith while having to follow Jewish traditions. This was not possible anymore, because God had a different plan. He used Paul and Peter to establish a Christian culture, a Christian way or manner of life and fellowship. Paul played an important role in how the Jewish and non-Jewish born again Christians learned to live with one another. Paul states that the Christian life begins by the following points:

- Living Sacrifices
- Do not live like the worldly people do
- Do not think higher of yourselves
- Everyone has a part
- Love
- Peace

According to Paul Christian life begins by being a living sacrifice — holy and pleasing to God. *"Therefore I urge you, brothers, in view of God's mercy, to offer your bodies as living sacrifices, holy and pleasing to God — this is your spiritual act of worship. Do not conform any longer to the patterns of this world, but be transformed by the renewing of your mind. Then you will be able to test and approve what God's will is- his good, pleasing and perfect will"* (Romans 12:1–2).

Christian life begins by becoming a living sacrifice. Normally, in the Old Testament, sacrifices had to do with the act of killing animals for the Lord or giving away grain and other things as an act of worshiping God. However, the Old Testament sacrifices were for one time use only. For example, if you killed a lamb, you could not re-use it next year. You would have to bring another lamb. Somehow, this is a bit easier than what Paul is saying. He is asking us to make ourselves the object of sacrifice, which is constantly alive, a living sacrifice. This is much harder than the rules in the Old Testament.

Living sacrifice is the act of worshiping God constantly. How to do this? By not conforming to the patterns of the world. In other words Paul is saying; now you are a Christian, changed through the light of the Gospel, therefore do not act like the worldly people. You are now different. Do not handle things based on people's worldly attitude, but through God's way. Since following the Gospel is a heavy assignment, this makes you a living sacrifice in Christ. Doing this will also reveal to you the pleasing will of the LORD in your life! What are these Christian attitudes that we have to follow? *"Do not think of yourself more highly than you ought, but rather think of yourself with sober judgment, in accordance with the measure of faith God has given you"* (Romans 12:3). This is one of the most important rules of Christian life. Arrogance is the killer of our faith. The Apostle Paul was urging the Church to put aside arrogance; this is exactly what the people of the world did and are still doing. We must remember that every one has his or her own function in the body of Christ, and that this does not make someone higher or lower than someone else. Paul mentions that we all need to function according to our gift, and doing this will bring unity in the body of Christ. These gifts include the following; spiritual gifts — *prophesying, teaching, leading;* social gifts — *encouraging, serving, hospitality;* financial gifts — *contributing;* organizational gifts — *governing and leadership* (Romans 12:6–8).

Another important point that Paul mentions is that we should live in such a way that our freedom in the Lord is not a stumbling block to other brothers / sisters in Christ who are weaker. There are some issues in faith that we keep private because God gives us the right and freedom to handle them, but this should not make others fall. For example, if you think drinking wine does not separate you from God, and you drink it without getting drunk and you control it, yet someone who is weaker with alcohol sees you, takes you as an example, drinks the wine and gets drunk, then you have not acted in love. Your "freedom in Christ" has tempted someone else. Therefore, Paul says to keep to ourselves what we believe are minor things and not make them public. *"Do not destroy the work of God for the sake of food. All food is clean, but it is wrong for man to eat anything that causes someone else to stumble. It is better not to eat meat or drink wine or do anything else that will cause your brother to fall. So whatever you believe about these things keep it between yourself and God"* (Romans 14:20–22).

Christian living also has to do with the measure of love we have towards each other, and Paul explains that love means honoring one another above ourselves (Romans 12:10). Also we have to be joyful in hope and patient in affliction, faithful in prayer, (Romans 12:12). Joy in hope gives us strength and power to continue in life. Patience gives us power to endure hardship, and faithful prayer gives us again hope to continue in life. This is like a circle continually at work in us.

"Eventually peace is the standard of our Christian living: "If it is possible, as far as it depends on you, live at peace with everyone. Do not take revenge, my friends, but leave room for God's wrath, for it is written: 'It is mine to revenge: I will repay,' says the Lord. On the contrary: 'If your enemy is hungry, feed him; if he is thirsty, give him something to drink. In doing this, you will heap burning coals on his head.' Do not be overcome by evil, but overcome evil with good" (Romans 12:17–21).

Peace is the greatest Christian strategy towards the world. If it depends on us we should be at peace with everyone. This is the essence of Christian faith. It is in acting in peace that we can gain the world for Christ, and gain the ability to answer evil with good and love our enemies. Those who do this are truly living sacrifices for God.

Submission to Government

Another important subject in Romans is the position of the Christians towards the local and national government. You have to imagine that in those days the Jews were ruled by Rome. Israel was under the dictatorship of the Roman Empire. There were many Jews living in Rome, and in those days the Jews were being discriminated against.

In the middle of this hostile situation, the good news of the gospel was able to unite the enemies and reconcile the Jews and Romans through faith in Christ. Paul advised the Christians to obey the rulers and the government. Paul says that every government is ordained by God whether good or bad! For example, we see in the Old Testament, that it was God Himself who ordained the Babylonians to attack Israel even though Babylonia was an evil state. Paul speaks of the authorities and state as God's servants, agents of wrath, who bring punishment to wrongdoers; this is why it is better to obey the authorities (Romans 13:4). Paul also urges us to do our duties such as paying taxes to the state (Romans 13:6–7).

Watch Out for False Teachers

Eventually, Paul warns the Christians to beware of false teachers, because these teachers cause division. In those days there were many false teachers, both from the Jewish Christian side and the gentiles' Christian side. They would come and mix different beliefs with Christianity and confuse people. These men were putting heavy loads on people and kept them from practicing what they had learned from the apostles. These false teachers could influence the naïve people.

"I urge you, brothers, to watch out for those who cause divisions and put obstacles in your way that are contrary to the teaching you have learned. Keep away from them. For such people are not serving our Lord Jesus Christ, but their own appetites. By smooth talk and flattery they deceive the minds of naïve people" (Romans 16:17–18). As you can see, these situations also occur today. There are leaders and teachers who, with their smooth talking, have fooled people in order to build their own kingdom and feed their own pockets at the cost of those who believe them.

Last Word

Indeed, the book of Romans is the short summary of the Old Testament and the Good News of the Gospel of Christ. This book is the foundation of many reformations in the body of Christ. Romans is the pioneering book of the modern Christian point of view. Romans deals with grace, with social justice, racial differences, and many other issues that our society now faces. Truly the writings of Paul have changed the path of Christianity and influenced the church during the past 2000 years.

Questions

1. What does Paul mean by "living sacrifices"? Explain.
2. What did Paul say concerning our position with the government and authorities?

Memorize

Romans 12:18

"If it is possible, as far as it depends on you, live at peace with everyone."

LESSON 4

I CORINTHIANS: *ORDERLY WORSHIP AND CHRISTIAN LIFE*

Lesson 4

I Corinthians: *Orderly Worship and Christian Life*

INTRODUCTION TO I CORINTHIANS

Corinth was and still is an important city in Greece, which is geographically located on the western side of Athens. We may compare the city of Corinth with modern day cities such as Amsterdam.

In Paul's time, Corinth had about 600,000 inhabitants, of which 400,000 were slaves. Corinth was a rich city. You may imagine that the city was mixed with many migrants who would live and work there as slaves of businessmen along with the native Greeks.

Corinth was famous for its Olympics and tradition, and Paul and his companions probably witnessed the Olympic Games in the years 40 and 51 while they were in Corinth. That is probably why Paul made a comparison between running a race and Christian life (1 Cor 9:24–27). Corinth, just like our modern day liberal cities, was a very open town. A lot of so-called "freedom activities" were tolerated, especially regarding sexuality.

Corinth was morally corrupt; practices like fornication and adultery had become a norm in their society. Prostitution was so common that in those days they had a term similar to "the Corinthian girl," which simply meant a prostitute. Or when men spoke about a "Corinthianised society," it means that the society became corrupt and perverted. Keeping this in mind, imagine that the Apostle Paul had evangelized these types of people in Corinth and the church he established there dealt with these types of social and moral problems.

Paul traveled to Corinth and stayed there for about a year. Since the church was not mature enough to support him financially, he was obligated to work. He partnered with Priscilla and Aquila and started a tent making business. Tradition says that he had a shop in one of the busiest streets in Corinth, giving him the chance to meet various types of people and evangelize to them. Later he stopped his business, because the Christians from Macedonia began to support him financially.

Paul taught in three various locations: first in the marketplace, second in the synagogue, and after that in private homes. As a result, he would gain many souls for Christ. Through Paul and Peter and other apostles, Christianity started to grow in Corinth. However, the church that Paul had established had many problems, such as immorality, order, and ethics due to immaturity in faith. After leaving Corinth, Paul moved to Ephesus and stayed there for a few years teaching and preaching the Gospel. While he was in Ephesus, another apostle called Apollos started to preach and teach in Corinth. This brought division and problems in Corinth and among the congregations of Paul. Some said they would follow Paul and some said they would follow Apollos. Because of all these social and ethical problems and disunity in the church, some of Paul's followers traveled to Ephesus and gave Paul a report about the situation in Corinth. The people who visited Paul were from the household of a believing and godly woman called Chloe. She informed Paul all about the terrible things happening there and handed over to him a letter that explained everything (1 Cor 1:11).

Lesson 4 / *Corinthians: Orderly Worship & Christian Life*

TODAY'S JOURNEY

1 Corinthians is a letter from Paul in response to what was happening in the Corinthian church. In this letter, Paul disciplined the believers and called them to unity, love, and order. 1 Corinthians is Paul's first letter to the people of Corinth. He systematically responded to all the matters explained to him in Chloe's letter. There were "six concerning matters," which Paul answered in 1 Corinthians, and by reading the letter or the book, you will notice the usage of the words: *"Now concerning..."* The book of Corinthians is the *"Now concerning..."* book.

- Concerning the marriage **(1 Cor 7:1)**.
- Concerning the virgins (unmarried people) **(1 Cor 7:25)**.
- Concerning food offered to idols **(1 Cor 8:1)**.
- Concerning spiritual gifts **(1 Cor 12:1)**.
- Concerning money contributions **(1 Cor 16:1)**.
- Concerning Apollos **(1 Cor 16:12)**.

Paul begins his letter in Chapter 1 with a call to unity: *"My brothers, some from Chloe's household have informed me that there are quarrels among you. What I mean is this: one of you says 'I follow Paul;' another, 'I follow Apollos' another 'I follow Cephas,' still another 'I follow Christ"* (1 Cor 1:11–12). From this statement we notice the mess going on there — the mess of disunity and dispute of who is right and who is wrong, whom to follow and whom not. The same is true today. Some say a certain man of God is good, and some say he is not. Paul gives us a great answer: *"Is Christ divided? Was Paul crucified for you? Were you baptized in the name of Paul?"* (1 Cor 1:13) In other words, it's all about Christ and the love of Christ! No big name evangelist, pastor, elder, bishop, prophet or apostle died for us. Only Jesus was ready to give His love for us and for all His enemies!

Concerning Marriage

1 Corinthians 7:1–24, deals with how Paul addressed the issue of marriage in response to Chloe's letter. Seemingly adulterous relationships were going on among the Corinthian believers in the church. Married men were having extra-marital affairs because of apparent dissatisfaction with their wives. On one side, it seemed that husbands were not responsibly taking good care of their wives, but on the other hand we see that wives likewise fell short in being sexually cooperative with their husbands. Therefore, this brought forth frustrations and eventually led to adulterous relationships.

Paul had a simple advice for them: *"the husband should fulfill his marital duty to his wife, and likewise the wife to her husband. The wife's body does not belong to her alone but to her husband. In the same way, the husband's body does not belong to him alone but to his wife. Do not deprive each other except by mutual consent and for a time, so that you may devote yourselves to prayer. Then come together again so that Satan will not tempt you because of your lack of self control"* (1 Cor 7:3–5). In other words, married couples should have a healthy sexual relationship with their partner so that they may not be tempted to do lustful and evil things. These matters need to be dealt with in the church. We have been ignoring these topics for a long time. What Paul also mentions is that sex is a matter of mutual agreement within the sacred walls of marriage and not through force.

Concerning Virgins (Unmarried)

From verse 25 in 1 Corinthians 7 Paul deals with the issue of singleness. The situation in Corinth was so bad that he asked people to remain single. If married remain married, if not married, stay single. This was his advice because he believed that a married person had many family burdens and could not work fully for God. However, this is a matter of choice. If a person desires a partner, then it is better to marry. In these passages between verse 25 to 39, you may read the instructions about choosing to marry someone or not. Also, it concerns widows and their rights to marry. Paul explicitly mentions that a Christian woman whose husband is dead may marry another man if he is a born again Christian, otherwise it is better that he or she stays single. (1 Cor 7: 39)

Concerning Food Offered to Idols

As you read 1 Corinthians 8, you may notice that some of the Corinthian believers would go to the temple and eat the food which was offered to gods and idols as a way of exercising their freedom in the Lord. Of course this act ridicules other beliefs and religions. Hence, Paul explicitly mentioned that even though idol worshiping is wrong and useless, we still should respect those who are weak in their faith by not humiliating them. There were newborn Christians from these groups who had to get used to the idea that idols' food was nothing but food, and if those who were strong in faith ate the idols' food the weak and the new believers would fall. What Paul meant is do not abuse your freedom at the cost of loosing your brother or sister who is weaker in faith: *"Be careful, however, that the exercise of your freedom does not become a stumbling block to the weak"* (1 Cor 8:9). And again he said: *"Therefore, if what I eat causes my brother to fall in sin, I will never eat meat again so that I will not cause him to fall"* (1 Cor 8:13).

Concerning Spiritual Gifts

Paul asked the church to exercise the gifts of the Holy Spirit, and claimed that everyone should know his or her place in the church both spiritually and naturally. These are the gifts of the Holy Spirit, as mentioned by Paul (1 Cor 12:7–10).

- Message of Wisdom
- Message of Knowledge
- Faith
- Healing
- Miracle making power
- Prophesy
- Distinguishing between spirits (Discernment)
- Tongues
- Interpretation of tongues

In 1 Corinthians 12 Paul explains all these gifts and urges people not to consider one more than the other, for we all have our place in His kingdom. In the church of Corinth it seems that those with certain gifts would look down on those with other gifts and this brought division among them.

In 1 Corinthians 13 Paul focuses on love, and elaborates on what love really means, explaining that the greatest gift of all is love, and that if the people do not have love for each other the way Christ showed us, they are nothing, even if they have great gifts. Paul mentions that the elements of love are the following (1 Cor 13:4–7):

- Patience
- Kindness
- Not boasting
- Not being proud
- Not easily angered
- Holding no record of wrong doings
- Not delighting in evil but rejoicing in truth
- Protection
- Trust

- Perseverance
- Love never fails, but eventually all other gifts vanish.

Concerning Contribution

In 1 Corinthians 9 Paul empties his heart concerning his hard life in Corinth, and reveals that even though he is an apostle he never received contributions from the Corinthian believers. That is why he starts working for his own food, until the believers from Macedonia began supporting him. Even though the Macedonians were not as rich as the Corinthians, they still supported Paul. He says that even though he had the full right to receive blessings, he did not! This hurt him the most because he did not receive any support for their sake, and they still lived immaturely and chaotically.

In 1 Corinthians 16 Paul admonished the believers in Corinth about financial dignity in collection: *"Now about the collection for God's people; do what I told the Galatians churches to do. On the first day of every week, each one of you should set aside a sum of money in keeping with his income, saving it up, so that when I come no collections will have to be made"* (1 Cor 16:1–2).

Concerning Apollos

In 1 Cor 16:12–18 Paul deals with the case of Apollos, and in his writing shows that he and Apollos are brothers, and that he even asked Apollos to come and visit the church in Corinth. From Paul's writing we understand that the problem was not between Paul and Apollos, but between the people who tried to compare the two brothers. We should be aware of this situation today and not compare men of God to each other in a wrong and competitive way, especially when they are friends or co-workers.

Miscellaneous Ethics

Paul also dealt with ethical matters such as women in the church, sexual immorality, church rules, and especially communion of the Lord's Supper.

- *Sexual immorality*

    "Flee from sexual immorality. All other sins a man commits are outside his body, but he who sins sexually sins against his own body. Do you not know that your body is a temple of the Holy Spirit, who is in you, whom you have received from God?" (1 Cor 6:18–19)

- *Lord's Supper*

    In those days some believers in Corinth seemed not to take the Lord's Supper seriously. They might drink wine and get so drunk that the Lord's Supper might lead them to commit more sins. In 1 Corinthians 11:17–34, Paul explains about the manners and ethics of having communion.

- *Women in Church*

    Paul restricts women to speak in the church (1 Cor 14:34). However, this was a matter specific to the Corinthian believers because these women were not discreet and would bring their domestic problems into the church, and with a loud voice discuss and quarrel with each other.

However, women can and must be involved in the ministry, and must minister out of being a woman and not act like a man, talk as a man, or do as a man. Imagine if I, being a man, started to act and preach as a woman, what would you think of me?

Questions

1. Explain in your own words the situation of the church in Corinth.
2. What are the elements of love?
3. What are the gifts of the Holy Spirit?

Memorize

1 Corinthians 8:9

"Be careful, however, that the exercise of your freedom does not become a stumbling block to the weak."

LESSON 5

II CORINTHIANS: SUFFERING FOR CHRIST

Lesson 5

II Corinthians: Suffering for Christ

TODAY'S JOURNEY

We learned in the previous lesson about the spiritual and moral situation of the Corinthian believers. Paul corrected the Corinthian believers in his first letter.

In his second letter, it seems that Paul's first letter had positive results, even though his letter was very harsh. Paul says in 2 Corinthians 7:8–9: *"Even if I caused you sorrow by my letter, I do not regret. Though I regret it-I see that my letter hurt you, but only for a while-yet now I am happy, not because you were made sorry, but because your sorrow led you to repentance. For you became sorrowful as God intended and so were not harmed in any way."*

Sometimes the truth is painful, but when it is revealed by the right person it has the ability to lead others to repentance. The body of Christ needs uncompromising men of God like Paul who never feared to tell the truth, even if it cost him his name, his reputation, and his life. Reading book of 2 Corinthians, you may notice a great change from Chapter 10 onwards. Chapters 1 to 9 were written in a praising and encouraging tone to the Corinthians, but this shifts into a hard and bitter self-defense concerning Paul's apostleship. We do not know the reason; however, some assume that the Corinthians did not receive two letters, but three.

Christian Ethics and Values

In 2 Corinthians 1–9, Paul deals with Christian ethics and values, and he also praises the Corinthians for being able to practice these.

- *Suffering: "Praise be to the God and Father of our Lord Jesus Christ, the Father of compassion and the God of all comfort, who comforts us in all our troubles, so that we can comfort those in any trouble with the comfort we ourselves have received from God"* (2 Cor 1:3–4).
  Suffering is a part of dying in Christ. It is in the suffering that we understand those who suffer! Use your suffering to ruin the kingdom of Satan by helping others who suffer.
- *Forgiveness: "if you forgive anyone I also will forgive him. And what I have forgiven-if there was anything to forgive-I have forgiven in the sight of Christ for your sake, in order that Satan might not outwit us. For we are not unaware of his schemes"* (2 Cor 2:10–11).

Lack of true forgiveness will lead us to be outwitted, deceived, confused, and tricked by Satan. Paul urged them to do so.

- *New Covenant & Freedom: "Now if the ministry that brought death, which was engraved in letters on stone, came with glory… If the ministry that condemns men is glorious, how much more glorious is the ministry that brings righteousness… Now the Lord is Spirit and where the Spirit of the Lord is, there is freedom…"* (2 Cor 3:7–17).
  According to Paul, the new law, or the new covenant, is not written on tablets of stone but on the tablets of our hearts

through the Spirit. This Spirit gives us freedom, and we shine the glory in us and through us to other people because we are children of the new covenant.
- *Do not partner with unbelievers:* "Do not be yoked with unbelievers..." (2 Cor 6:14–18).

Paul urges us not to partner with those who do not believe, especially on a business and marriage level, for there is not alliance between the world and Kingdom of God.

- *Money:* "Remember this: Whoever sows sparingly will also reap sparingly, and whoever sows generously will also reap generously. Each man should give what he has decided in his heart to give, not reluctantly or under compulsion, for God loves a cheerful giver. And God is able to make all grace abound in you, so that in all things at all times, having all that you need, you will abound in every good work" (2 Cor 9:6–8).

The secret of blessing is in generous giving, not out of pressure and force but out of conviction. A generous giver from the heart will reap abundantly. We do not need people to convince us, we need the Holy Spirit to convince us, people only confirm to us.

Paul's Self-Defense

In those days, there were "super" apostles in Corinth who were ridiculing Paul. According to them, Paul had no charisma and his writings made no sense. They claim Paul's sight is weak, and he does not deserve to be called as an apostle. However, from 2 Corinthians 10–13 Paul defends himself in love, arguing that he is a true apostle who will not compromise his teachings with fake ones. He also warns them of the false and tricky apostles.

Questions

1. What does Paul mean by engraved letters on the stone in 2 Cor 3:7–11?
2. Read 2 Corinthians 10 and 11 and write down the sufferings Paul went through for the sake of the gospel.
3. Why did the "super" apostles disrespect Paul?

Memorize

2 Corinthians 9:6

"Remember this: Whoever sows sparingly will also reap sparingly, and whoever sows generously will also reap generously."

LESSON 6

GALATIANS: *THE TRUTH OF THE GOSPEL*

Lesson 6

GALATIANS: *THE TRUTH OF THE GOSPEL*

INTRODUCTION TO GALATIANS

Contrary to the books of Romans and Corinthians, the book of Galatians is not named after a city, but after a whole region. Galatia was a province in contemporary central Turkey, which belonged to the Roman Empire. Paul wrote this book in the form of a letter to the churches in Galatia. He established these churches through his ministry. The important cities in Galatia were Antioch, Lystra, Derbe, Iconium, Pessinus and Ancyra.

Paul wrote his letter to the Galatians while he was in Corinth. Galatians was a book of reformation back then for the Jewish Christian church. Later, the book of Galatians was used during the Reformation era in the 15th century. During that time, Protestantism was rising up against the hypocrisy of the Roman Catholic Church and marked by a period of Christian faith reformation. Galatians is an answer to the hypocrisy and self-righteousness in the body of Christ back then and today.

In this book, Paul uses hard language, even harder than what he used in his letters to the Corinthians. Paul was perplexed because of what was going on among the churches in Galatia.

The Galatian church had experienced revival among the gentiles who formerly believed in the Hellenic religions and customs; later they gave their lives to Christ through the ministry of Paul.

Just after Paul left Galatia, certain apostles and teachers (especially among the Jewish Christians) rose among the people in the church who were teaching the Gospel based on the flesh, which means that a gentile would never be saved if he did not follow the laws and customs of the Jewish, such as being circumcised, keeping the Sabbath, and many other rules. This confused many people and it made Paul furious. Paul wrote:

"I am astonished that you are so quickly deserting the one who called you by the grace of Christ and are turning to a different Gospel-which is really no gospel at all. Eventually some people are throwing you into confusion and trying to pervert the gospel of Christ. But even if we or even an angel from heaven should preach a gospel other than the one we preached to you, let him be eternally condemned... 'You foolish Galatians! Who has bewitched you? Before your very eyes Jesus Christ was clearly portrayed as crucified. I would like to learn just one thing from you: did you receive the Spirit by observing the Law or by believing what you heard? Are you so foolish? After beginning with the Spirit, are you now trying to attain your goal by human effort'" (Galatians 1:6–8, 3:1–3).

TODAY'S JOURNEY

Flesh Versus Spirit

As we read in Galatians, there are two things that are continually in battle: the flesh versus the Spirit. The Apostle Paul was warning the Church that following the flesh in place of the Spirit couldn't save man. By 'flesh' he meant: following cultural or religious rules and regulations in order to be saved or to achieve things in life through the flesh.

"All who rely on observing the law are under a curse, for it is written: cursed is everyone who does not continue to obey everything written in the Book of the law ... Clearly no one is justified before God by the law, because, the righteous will live by faith ... The law is not based on faith; on contrary, the man who does these things will live by them ... Christ redeemed us from the curse of the law by becoming a curse for us, for it is written: cursed is everyone who is hung on a tree" (Deut. 27:26, Heb. 2:4, Lev. 18:5, Galatians 3:10–13).

The Apostle Paul was explaining to the church that in the Old Testament times, people lived by the law and by the flesh, and that all things in the law are shadows of the things to come through Christ and His Spirit. Paul tried to explain that man should not be justified through the law, but rather through faith in Jesus Christ. This means we should live by the Spirit and not by the law. Since we live by faith through the Spirit we become the spiritual children of Abraham and therefore co-heirs with him (Read Galatians 3:15–18).

- **Natural Children — Spiritual Children**

  Since we are all children of God through Jesus Christ, then nationality and culture has no more effect in our relationship with God and with one another. *"There is neither Jew nor Greek, slave or free, male or female, for you are all one in Christ. If you belong to Christ, then you are Abraham's seed, and heirs according to the promise"* (Galatians 3:28–29).

- **Slavery — Freedom**

  "It is for freedom that Christ has set us free. Stand firm, then, and do not let yourself be burdened again by the yoke of slavery" (Galatians 5:1). Paul was saying that following the fleshly part of the law, culture, traditions, and other customs will make us slaves to religion. We are free in the Spirit to live by the Spirit, which was given to us by Christ.

However, this freedom must not be abused nor be harmful to others. We should understand that the law of Moses had two aspects: the spiritual aspects and physical aspects. Paul was not against the spiritual aspects of the law. What does the spiritual aspect of the law mean? It refers to laws such as "Do not lie," "Do not steal," "Do not murder," etc. The physical aspect of the law refers to being circumcised, going to church on Saturday, washing the body in a certain way, etc.

- **Human effort — Spiritual effort**

    Eventually, Paul challenged the Galatians not to live their lives on their own human efforts, values, standards, or understanding, but wait on the Lord and move according to the Spirit and His will. Since Sarah was barren and could not wait upon the promise of God, she lived her life based on human custom and understanding. Therefore (according to her will, not God's will), she asked Abraham to sleep with Hagar so that through Hagar she would get a child for Abraham. As a result Ishmael was born into slavery, while Isaac was the promised son who was born through the spiritually directed lifestyle (Galatians 4:21–31). This is a huge lesson for all of us. Let our lives be directed by the Holy Spirit and not by our fleshly efforts.

Questions

1. What does it mean to be free from the Law?
2. Read the whole book of Galatians and find one or two things that made Paul furious (quote the scriptures).

Memorize

Galatians 5:1

"It is for freedom that Christ has set us free. Stand firm, then, and do not let yourself be burdened again by a yoke of slavery."

LESSON 7

EPHESIANS PART I:
THE BOOK OF GOD'S CALL

Lesson 7

EPHESIANS PART I: *THE BOOK OF GOD'S CALL*

INTRODUCTION TO EPHESIANS

While Paul was in prison either in Rome or in Caesarea, he wrote a letter directed to the Ephesians. This book became one of the important books in the New Testament.

In Ephesians Paul emphasizes important issues such as the equal opportunity for receiving salvation by the Jews and the Gentiles, and both form the body of Christ, which is the Church. Ephesians was written to the believers in the city of Ephesus. In the book of Acts, this city is mentioned. In Acts 19, Paul arrives in Ephesus and notices that the believers were not baptized, and so he challenges them to receive the Holy Spirit. He then lays his hand on them, and they were all filled with Holy Spirit and started to pray in tongues. Some believed Paul evangelized to the Ephesian Jews first in the synagogues. Paul took his disciples and had discussions daily in the lecture hall of Tyranmus for two years and through this the Jews and Greeks living in Asia heard the Gospel. Ephesus experienced great revival through Paul's ministry, which was followed by signs and wonders. Great miracles took place and people everywhere began to talk about Jesus. This was the city where Paul's handkerchiefs were used as a contact point of healing and casting out demons. The revival was so great that the local businesses of those who traded in handicrafts of gods, goddesses, and shrines were bankrupt. There is one story of a well-known silversmith who received a great income from making shrines of Artemis and was affected to the point of bankruptcy. Even a great riot broke out due to Paul's ministry in Ephesus.

The book of Ephesians is crucial because it deals with the fundamental issues of the Church as being the body of Christ. It also deals with how the members of the body of Christ should relate to each other and how the Church as a whole is related to Christ. Finally, the book discusses how the Church should fight the battle against evil forces, principalities, and the powers of the air.

Another important subject in this book is the establishment of God's authority within the church, the five-fold ministry. In summary of the book of Ephesians, this book is the handbook of our calling. It deals with the call of God in every individual's life and at the same time the call of God for the church as the body. Ephesians is the book of God's Calling.

TODAY'S JOURNEY

One Body

The Apostle Paul emphasizes that we all, through the blood of Jesus, have become united in Christ. Therefore Christianity is not exclusive for the Jews or the circumcised. In those days, whether they should accept the Gentile Christians into their gatherings was a great issue among Jewish Christians. Again, most Jewish Christians thought that Jesus Christ came only for the Jews.

"For he himself (Jesus Christ) is our peace, who has made the two one and has destroyed the barrier, the dividing wall of hostility, by abolishing in his flesh the law with its commandments and

regulations. His purpose was to create in himself one new man out of two, thus making peace, and in this one body to reconcile both of them to God through the cross, by which he put to death their hostility"* (Ephesians 2:14–16).

It is interesting to know that during Jesus' time, on the outer wall of Herod's Temple, there was an inscription in Greek warning the gentiles not to enter the temple's inner court under the threat of death penalty. Paul speaks in Ephesians that Christ has broken down the wall that kept the gentiles from the house of God. We are now one body in Christ, and there is no difference between a Jewish and a Non Jewish believer.

Call and Purpose

In Ephesians 1, Paul is teaching us that we are a chosen people, the called out ones, and that we are predestined according to His plan; in other words, He has called us into His will and purpose. Then in chapter two he says: *"For we are God's workmanship, created in Christ Jesus to do good works, which God prepared for us in advance to do"* (Ephesians 2:10). In other words, your job is already assigned; you are created for a purpose and that is to do and be good in whatever God has called you to. Life, however, is a matter of choice; if we choose to be removed from the will of God and follow our own desires, God will not force His will on us. We must realize that we are created to do the will of God here on earth, and if we do not, we are outside God's will and therefore are vulnerable.

God's Established Authorities

"It was he who gave some to be apostles, some to be prophets, some to be evangelists, and some to be pastors and teachers, to prepare God's people for works of service so that the body of Christ may be built up until we all reach unity in faith and in

knowledge of the Son of God and become mature, attaining to the whole measure of the fullness of Christ" (Ephesians 4:11–13).

Ephesians is well known for the passage we just read. These verses call for the body of Christ to understand Kingdom authority and the establishment of God's government in the Church.

Paul spoke of five major ministries: the ministry of the apostle, prophet, evangelist, pastor, and teacher. In order to understand the function of these ministries, we must first look at the shape of God's Kingdom here on earth. This kingdom was established by Jesus Christ, continues today, and will continue forever, until Christ comes back for the second time. However, in the Lord's Prayer, Jesus teaches us to pray: "our Father in heaven hallowed be your name, your kingdom come, your will be done here on earth as it is in heaven..." (Matthew 6:9). This means that we as Christians have to proclaim the Kingdom of God and do our best to establish God's Kingdom until Christ's return.

We have the ministries of apostles, prophets, evangelists, pastors and teachers. These are God's anointed people, so that they can reach unity and maturity in the body of Christ. God's people are the ambassadors of Christ in their community and the marketplace or in the various fields where they live and work. Church then, is God's embassy in every community or marketplace, village, city or country, or any place where Christians are represented. Understanding this picture helps us understand the function of the five-fold ministry.

Five-Fold Ministry

What is the actual role of the five-fold ministry? 1. Apostles 2. Prophets 3. Evangelists 4. Pastors 5. Teachers. All of these offices are crucial in the Kingdom of God, which are discussed in the following paragraphs.

First, we should understand that every office is meant for today. Many people say that the office of the apostle or the prophet is not relevant for our time. They argue that these offices were only meant for the time of Jesus' disciples and during the period of the book of Acts. Likewise, some say that the prophets were only relevant for Old Testament times. However, there are no difficulties in recognizing the office of the evangelist, pastor, and teacher, and the Church should accept the ministries of the apostle and prophet as well. It's interesting to note that the word apostle is mentioned over 90 times in the New Testament; whereas the title of pastor is mentioned only a few times.

Apostles

According to C. Peter Wagner, an apostle is a Christian leader gifted, taught, commissioned and sent by God with authority to establish foundational government of the Church within an assigned sphere of ministry by hearing what the Holy Spirit is saying to the Church by setting things in order accordingly for the growth and maturity of the Church. *The ministry of the apostle is for today. Without the apostle's ministry, there will be chaos in the body of Christ. Apostles are generals and fathers and as such, they make sure that the people under their care will find their call and destiny in the Kingdom of God and fulfill them.*

Today, the Church should recognize this important and crucial ministry. The book of Malachi ends with a very important statement: *"See, I will send you the prophet Elijah before that great and dreadful day of the LORD comes. He will turn the hearts of the fathers to their children and the hearts of the children to their fathers; or else I will come and strike the land with a curse"* (Malachi 4:5–6). In these verses the word "fathers" can be likened to "apostles." The Church should be covered and directed by apostles. One or two apostles should cover every Christian ministry.

In other chapters I discuss in detail the ministry of the apostles and how we should find and recognize true apostles.

Prophets

Prophets reveal the Father's heart and mind to the Church. The ministry of the prophet is like a compass, which helps us go the direction God wants us to go. In Ephesians 2:20 Paul says *"build on the foundation of the apostles and prophets, with Christ Jesus himself as the chief cornerstone."* The prophet's guidance makes the church prosper, and the ministry of the prophet and the apostle are strongly linked and interconnected. Prophets should have an apostle to cover them and they both should work alongside each other. Prophets reveal God's will and direction both to the Church and to individuals.

Evangelists

The ministry of the evangelist is crucial. It is the evangelists who import people and souls from darkness to light. Evangelists preach the Gospel, for God has given them grace and special charisma to attract people and to bring them into the Kingdom.

Pastors

Once souls are saved, they need a place to grow. This happens in the local church and in fellowship with believers. Pastors are shepherds; they care for people, love, and nurture them. Pastors guide the people in their daily affairs and heal them from their inner battles. Pastors are caring and loving

Teachers

The work of the teacher is to teach believers the biblical standard of life. Knowledge is essential to the Body of Christ. Teachers are like the immune system of the Body of Christ; they teach us to be alert, especially towards false ministers who manipulate and abuse people. The relationship between the manipulator and the manipulated is a co-dependant one. If we do not allow ourselves to be manipulated, then there will be no manipulators. We allow ourselves to be manipulated because we lack knowledge. God said in the book of Hosea, *"my people are destroyed from lack of knowledge"* (Hosea 4:6). Further, lack of knowledge comes because we lack true teachers. If there are true teachers in a church or ministry, there will be no manipulators because people will be aware of the truth.

Finally

Ephesians emphasizes relationships within the body of Christ. In Ephesians 5 and 6 Paul explains the relationships between husband and wife, children and parents, employers and employees.

In the husband-wife relationship he explains that the husband should love his wife as Christ loved the Church and the wife should love the husband as the Church loves Christ. This will help the family prosper.

He also explains that children should obey their parents so that they may prosper. This is also a promise in the Ten Commandments; *"Children, obey your parents in the Lord, for this is right. Honor your father and mother ..."* which is the first commandment with a promise *"that it may go well with you and that you may enjoy long life on the earth"* (Ephesians 6:1–3, Deuteronomy 5:16). Notice that Paul said "obey your parents in the Lord." This has two meanings: first of all, he mentions *'in the Lord.'* This means that we have to put God and His laws first, and in that framework obey our parents. Imagine if our parents lead us to sins like lying, stealing, or keeping us from believing; should we then still obey? No! We must obey in the framework of the Lord.

Secondly, *"in the Lord"* means our spiritual fathers and mothers, those who lead us and shepherd us into green pastures. Obeying them will bless us and add to our lives. At the same time Paul urges fathers and mothers not to exasperate their children; rather, they should bring them to the Lord and guide them.

Questions

1. Paul said in Ephesians 2:14: *"for he himself (Jesus Christ) is our peace, who has made the two one and has destroyed the barrier, the dividing wall of hostility, by abolishing in his flesh the law with its commandments and regulations."* What does he mean by that? Define the dividing wall, and explain why Paul uses it as an illustration.
2. Explain in detail the functions of the five-fold ministry.

Memorize

Ephesians 4:11–13

"It was He who gave some to be apostles, some to be prophets, some to be evangelists, and some to be pastors and teachers to prepare God's people for works of service, so that the body of Christ may be built up until we reach unity in faith and in the knowledge of the Son of God and become mature, attaining to the whole measure of the fullness of Christ."

LESSON 8

EPHESIANS PART II:
SPIRITUAL WARFARE

Lesson 8

EPHESIANS PART II: SPIRITUAL WARFARE

TODAY'S JOURNEY

One of the most famous scriptures in Ephesians is found in Chapter 6:10–18: *"Finally be strong in the Lord and in his mighty power. Put on the full armor of God so that you can take your stand against the devil's schemes. For our struggle is not against flesh and blood, but against the rulers, against the authorities, against the powers of this dark world and against the spiritual forces of evil in the heavenly realms. Therefore put on the full armor of God, so that when the day of evil comes, you may be able to stand your ground, and after you have everything, to stand. Stand firm then, with the belt of truth buckled around your waist, with the breastplate of righteousness in place, and with your feet fitted with the readiness that comes from the gospel of peace. In addition to all this, take up the shield of faith with which you can extinguish all the flaming arrows of the evil one. Take the helmet of salvation and the sword of the Spirit, which is the word of God. And pray in the Spirit on all occasions with all kinds of prayers and requests. With this in mind, be alert and always keep on praying for all the saints."*

Many Christians are continuously in battle; in our terms we call it spiritual warfare. The scripture we just read is a guideline on how to fight against Satan and his forces. Before we analyze what the Apostle Paul mentions in Ephesians 6, we must first realize that from the time we were born, and especially when we are born again, we are continuously in battle. These battles require decision-making and there are two ways to go about it; the first is God's Way and His plan for us and the other is Satan's way and his plan for our lives. Life itself is a matter of choice. What we choose determines the course of our lives. If we choose God and His son Christ Jesus, then the course of our life is in His will and plan, but if we choose our own way, i.e., outside the will and plan of God, then we are on our own and vulnerable to Satan's schemes.

The battle forms a stronger level when we give our lives to Christ, because then Satan has lost his power over us and he tries by all ways and means to bring us back where we were before — back to our spiritual Egypt where we were captive under his power. Just like every battle and war, there are weapons to be used. What kind of weapons are used in this battle? What are our weapons to fight Satan's forces? In Ephesians Chapter 6, Paul teaches us the weaponry of God's spiritual warfare: *"Finally be strong in the Lord and in his mighty power. Put on the full armor of God so that you can take your stand against the devil's schemes. For our struggle is not against flesh and blood, but against the rulers, against the authorities, against the powers of this dark world and against the spiritual forces of evil in the heavenly realms."*

Paul encourages believers to put on the full armor of God in order to fight the devil's schemes. He then emphasizes that our fight is not against flesh and blood; in other words, people are not our enemy. Many people make a mistake and take a person or even a nation as their enemy. Remember that Jesus was not the enemy of the sinner; He was the enemy of sin. Jesus hated prostitution but loved the prostitute; He forgave the woman caught in adultery and commanded her not to sin anymore. What Paul the Apostle is trying to teach us is that we should not fight against flesh and blood, but against the spiritual force and power that causes the flesh to sin. What are these forces? Recall Ephesians 6, *"For our struggle is not against flesh and blood, but against the rulers, against the authorities, against the powers of this dark world and against the spiritual forces of evil in the heavenly realms."* Satan has appointed devils and demons from various ranks and types to rule certain areas, territories, families, companies, and nations.

It should not surprise Christians to notice that in certain families there are curses. For example, every male person in the family dies by accident, or in certain geographical territories we can feel the presence of the spiritual forces that cause people to use drugs and indulge in alcohol. Therefore, Paul challenges us to fight these spiritual forces. How? *"Therefore put on the full armor of God, so that when the day of evil comes, you may be able to stand your ground..."* The armor that Paul mentions is spiritual armor. Putting on this armor enables us to stand firm in the evil days of hardship and darkness. Paul took his description of spiritual armor from the physical Roman armor and gave it spiritual meaning.

The Armor

- **Belt of Truth:** *Stand firm then, with the belt of truth buckled around your waist.* Normally belts are buckled around the waist. The waist is the balance of the body. Having a weak waist means not being able to stand firm. Paul spoke about the Belt of Truth; this is the belt of the simplicity of the Gospel truth. By having the pure truth, which comes through the Word of God in our lives, nothing will be able to shake us and make us insecure in life. Our foundation should be based on God's truth, which is found in His words. Being rooted in the truth of God makes us like a strong tree — never shaking, never trembling.

- **The Breastplate of Righteousness:** *with the breastplate of righteousness in place.* Breastplates are meant to protect the heart and the surrounding organs of the heart. Paul mentions the breastplate of righteousness, which is God's righteousness in us. Practicing it will protect our hearts from all types of evil.
- **The Shield of Faith:** *take up the shield of faith with which you can extinguish all the flaming arrows of the evil one.* The shield's function is to protect the fighter from the poisonous arrows and swords of the enemies. In the spiritual battle, the shield of faith functions likewise. We need faith to move on during the hard times of life. We need faith to do the impossible. In this context, faith also means trust in God. By entrusting our anxieties and worries into God's hand, we are building a shield of faith. This shield will protect us from the spiritual arrows, which are the sudden events and unexpected attacks in our lives.
- **The Helmet of Salvation:** *take the helmet of salvation.*

  Why would Paul use the combination of helmet and salvation? Helmet protects the head and face. As a Christian we make mistakes most of the time and because of that, a whole battle goes on in our minds (heads). This makes it easy for the enemy to accuse us either through our friends, people or even ourselves.

  Paul uses the combination of helmet and salvation because salvation is God's grace and we live by God's grace. Therefore it is God's salvation, which comes through His grace that we can protect our minds from accusations, guilty feelings and failure.
- **The Sword of the Spirit:** *the sword of the Spirit, which is the word of God.*

The word of God is not only there to be read, but also to be used. The word of God is a sword, which cuts everything and those trying to attack us. For example, when sickness comes, we can use the word of God and say: "it is written, that by His blood I am healed" and as you stand on this Word and as you speak it out it will penetrate into the sickness, by faith. Just like Jesus, when Satan tempted him, He consequently answered Satan with: "it is written…"

- **Pray in the Spirit:** *and pray in the Spirit on all occasions with all kinds of prayers and requests. With this in mind, be alert and always keep on praying for all the saints."* The last strongest weapon is praying in the Spirit in all occasions. We have to pray continually. In other words, our lives must be a life of prayer. By praying in the Spirit and better yet, if we have the gift of tongues, we are then kept alert and the Holy Spirit can reveal the secrets and schemes of the enemy.

Questions

1. Describe the Armor of God as mentioned by Paul in Ephesians 6: 10–18.
2. Describe and discuss some spiritual warfare you have been going through and how you overcome it.

Memorize

Ephesians 6:12

"For our struggle is not against flesh and blood, but against the rulers, against the authorities, against the powers of this dark world and against the spiritual forces of evil in the heavenly realms."

LESSON 9

PHILIPPIANS: THE BOOK OF JOY

Lesson 9

PHILIPPIANS: THE BOOK OF JOY

INTRODUCTION TO PHILIPPIANS

Philippians is written during Paul's first imprisonment in Rome, shortly after he wrote the books of Ephesians and Colossians. Philippians is one of the most personal letters that Paul wrote. Paul had a good relationship with the church in Philippi, an important city in Macedonia. Paul established this church and the majority of them were converted gentiles.

The Philippians were very generous. They planted seed into Paul's ministry when he was arrested in Rome. The Philippians sent Epaphroditus to Rome to deliver financial assistance to Paul. Epaphroditus' journey was so dangerous and risky that he almost died from illness. Paul praised these acts of love in his letter to the Philippians. The believers in Philippi also donated huge amount of funds for the suffering church in Jerusalem.

TODAY'S JOURNEY

Joy in Partnership

In Philippians Paul repeatedly expresses his joy and requests the Philippians do likewise. In his letter he mentions the word joy more than 15 times. What would cause Paul to rejoice and speak of joy to the Philippians? In the coming paragraphs we will analyze the cause of Paul's joy and what the apostle understands as Christian joy. The opening verses of Philippians begin with joy: *"I thank my God every time I remember you. In all my prayers for all of you, I always pray with **joy** because of your partnership in the gospel from the first day until now, being confident of this, that he who began a good work in you will carry it on to completion until the day of Christ Jesus"* (Philippians 1:3–6, emphasis added)

Paul's joy came through the partnership in the Gospel that the Philippian believers offered him. This partnership was not only financial but also emotional. The Philippians were concerned with the matters of Paul's ministry; they were supporting the apostle so that the gospel could be preached through him. There is great joy when believers begin supporting the Gospel with their finances. The Kingdom of God needs finances, and learning how we should deal with tithing is essential.

In Philippians 4, from verse 14 to the end, Paul once again thanks the Philippians for their gift and reminds them that when he set out from Macedonia, not one church supported him except them. He mentions that God will take notice of this generous act. Paul rejoices because he knew the condition of the Philippian believers; they were not rich and yet they supported Paul's ministry.

Joy Because Christ is Preached

Paul mentions that some preach Christ out of envy and rivalry, but others preach out of goodwill. However, what happens in the end is that Christ is being preached and no one can stop this Gospel from being proclaimed. He then added: *"And because of this I rejoice"* (Philippians 1:18). A true believer rejoices in seeing that the Gospel is being preached; this joy comes from the heart and is not man-made.

Joy in Suffering

Paul also mentions that he rejoices in his suffering: *"Yes, and I will continue to rejoice, for I know that through your prayers and the help given by the Spirit of Jesus Christ, what has happened to me will turn out for my deliverance [salvation]"* (Philippians 1:19).

Imagine that Paul was imprisoned because of the Gospel. He was in chains in Rome and was waiting for his verdict; he was not sure what the verdict would be, and yet he was rejoicing in prison. Even in chains he rejoiced: *"For me to live is Christ and to die is gain"* (Philippians 1:21). In other words, for him it did not matter whether he stayed or went to Christ; in both ways he learned to rejoice.

Joy is a matter of learning. We have to train ourselves to rejoice, even in the most difficult times in our lives when we suffer and go through pain — especially when it is for Christ.

Joy in Unity & Fellowship

"If you have any encouragement from being united with Christ, if any comfort from his love, if any fellowship with the Spirit, if any tenderness and compassion, **then make my joy complete** *by being like-minded, having the same love, being one in spirit and purpose. Do nothing out of selfish ambition or vain conceit, but in humility consider others better than yourselves. Each of you should look not only to your own interests, but also to the interest of others"* (Philippians 2:1–4, emphasis added).

Paul urges the believers to make his joy complete by being united, having one purpose, and not acting out of selfish ambitions. This brings joy in the heart of the believers and their leaders. This is the essence of Christian faith, so that Christ will be displayed and preached, not only by words but also by deeds.

JOY IN THE LORD

"Finally, my brothers, rejoice in the Lord!" (Philippians 3:1) In Chapter 3, Paul again asks the believers to rejoice in the Lord. What Paul means by rejoicing in the Lord is to take joy in knowing Christ and the power of His resurrection (verse 10). What is the use of all knowledge and material possessions, if one does not know Christ and the power of His resurrection? Knowing these two things can bring us through in life. Once we know the power of Christ's resurrection it opens the doors of breakthroughs and blessings. However, right after that he mentions "the fellowship of sharing in his suffering" (verse 10). In other words, knowing Him and the power of His resurrection is not the only reason to rejoice, but also rejoice in His suffering and the persecution that comes because of following Christ. Even in this there is reason to rejoice. Jesus said: *"Blessed are you when men hate you, when they exclude you and insult you and reject your name as evil, because of the Son of Man. Rejoice in that day and leap for joy, because great is your reward in heaven. For that is how their fathers treated the prophets"* (Luke 6:22–23).

Finally, Paul mentions to rejoice in the Lord by not worrying, and through prayer rejoice in the Lord: *"Rejoice in the Lord always, I will say it again: Rejoice! ... Do not be anxious about anything, but in everything by prayer and petition with thanksgiving present your request to God"* (Philippians 4:4–6). In other words, give thanks to God in all situations, and with gladness and gentleness, ask God your requests. This is the secret of a joyful Christian life.

Other Matters

In the book of Philippians there are also important and famous statements from the Apostle Paul that are regularly used in sermons and other messages. For instance, in Philippians 2:6–11, Paul emphasizes that Christ is exalted above everything, His

Name is above every name, and eventually every knee will bow unto Him. This is a true statement, yet at the same time quite prophetic. Soon after Paul's death and the persecutions of many Christians, a day came in which even the Roman Empire bowed down to the Gospel of Christ. Ever since there has been no power on earth capable of withstanding the power of Christ; even communism collapsed and bowed down to Christ. This should give us hope and joy that no matter what and how, in all circumstances, Jesus Christ, who is in us, will make us the ultimate winner.

Questions

1. Describe the joy that Paul was suggesting to the Philippian believers.
2. Why is the book of Philippians the most intimate of Paul's letters?

Memorize

Philippians 4:6

"Do not be anxious about anything, but in everything by prayer and petition, with thanksgiving, present your requests to God."

LESSON 10

COLOSSIANS:
PAUL'S DEFENSE

Lesson 10

COLOSSIANS: *PAUL'S DEFENSE*

INTRODUCTION TO COLOSSIANS

Colossians was written to the church in the city of Colosse, situated in what is now current Turkey, while Paul was imprisoned either in Rome or Caesarea. Colosse was an important city because it was situated on the commercial route between the West and the East. Many goods were being transported into this place which boosted the regional economy. A man named Epaphras, whom Paul called his "dear fellow servant," most probably evangelized the Colossian believers. It seems Epaphras was one of the disciples of Paul or he was converted into Christianity through Paul in Ephesus.

In Colossians, Paul deals with various aspects of the Christian faith. However, he was mostly concerned about false doctrines that entered the Colossian church; issues such as angel worshiping, denying of Godhead of Christ, etc. He also instructed the believers to live a correct Christian life.

TODAY'S JOURNEY

Christ the Image of God

Paul writes: *"He is the image of the invisible God, the firstborn over all creation. For by him all things were created: things in heaven and on earth, visible and invisible, whether thrones or powers or rulers or authorities; all things were created by him and for him. He is before all things, and in him all things hold together. And he is the head of the body, the Church; he is the beginning and the firstborn from among the dead, so that in everything he might have the supremacy. For God was pleased to have all his fullness dwell in him, and through him to reconcile to himself all things, whether things on earth or things in heaven, by making peace through his blood, shed on the cross"* (Colossians 1:15–20). These verses indicate important facts:

a. Christ is the image of God
b. He is the first born over all creation
c. He created all things in heaven and on earth, the visible and invisible
d. He has the supremacy
e. God's being dwells in Him
f. Through Him the creation is reconciled to God

These facts simply indicate that Jesus Christ is God and He is the visible image of God. God who was invisible and untouchable is now available and tangible! We should also realize that even before Adam or any of the angels were formed or created Jesus existed, as all things were in Him and made by Him.

One of the teachings of the false teachers was that Christ is not God. Many questioned His deity, and therefore Paul wrote these words to tackle the issue of the false teachers who professed this false doctrine. Paul also taught that Christ is the first-born among the dead! Which dead? Were there no dead raised into life before? Many times in the Old Testament the prophets raised people from the dead. Why then would Paul speak about the first born among the dead? He did not only mean the physical death, but the spiritual death which came through sin. Jesus Christ was the first of many who rose from the dead in victory and power. For this reason, Paul speaks of being a new creation, because in Christ a new nature of man was born.

Christ Defeated Satan

"When you were dead in your sins and in the uncircumcision of your sinful nature, God made you alive with Christ. He forgave us all our sins, having canceled the written code, with its regulations, that was against us and that stood opposed to us; he took it away, nailing it to the cross. And having disarmed the powers and authorities, he made a public spectacle of them, triumphing over them by the cross" (Colossians 2:13–15). This is important information for believers to know. What did Jesus accomplish through His death? He first gave us life; He forgave us by canceling the judgment of the Law upon us (the written code). He then **disarmed** the powers and authorities! He publicly ridiculed them! Jesus, through His death, took away all Satan's weapons. Satan is already disarmed! What were Satan's arms and weapons?

a. Accusations (Jesus destroyed any accusation)
b. Fear (Jesus took all the fear Satan tried to put on us)
c. Illness & Curses (By His blood we are healed)

There are of course many weapons Satan can use against us, but we should never forget that Jesus disarmed Satan, so why fear?

Characteristics of the False Teachers

Paul then warned the believers of the characteristics of false teachers: See to it that no one **takes you captive through hollow and deceptive philosophy**, which depends on human tradition and the basic principles of this world rather than on Christ (Colossians 2:8, emphases added). Also, from verse 16 to 23, Paul describes false teachers as the following:

"Therefore do not let anyone judge you by what you eat or drink, or with regard to a religious festival, a New Moon celebration or a Sabbath day. These are a shadow of the things that were to come; the reality, however, is found in Christ. Do not let anyone who delights in false humility and the worship of angels disqualify you for the prize. Such a person goes into great detail about what he has seen, and his unspiritual mind puffs him up with idle notions. He has lost connection with the Head, from whom the whole body, supported and held together by its ligaments and sinews, grows as God causes it to grow. Since you died with Christ to the basic principles of this world, why, as though you still belonged to it, do you submit to its rules: 'Do not handle! Do not taste! Do not touch!' These are all destined to perish with use, because they are based on human commands and teachings. Such regulations indeed have an appearance of wisdom, with their self-imposed worship, their false humility and their harsh treatment of the body, but they lack any value in restraining sensual indulgence" (Colossians 2:16–23).

The techniques of the false teachers are as follows:

a. Hallow and deceptive philosophies- they take you captive!
b. Judgmental on food and religious festivals
c. False humility
d. Great details of what they saw in visions — false wisdom
e. Angel worship
f. Harsh treatment of the body

False teachers captivate their audience by deceptive philosophies. On the other hand, there also exist false researchers within the church who can philosophize seemingly biblical issues in such a way that people may be deceived!

They also judge on fleshly matters and judge the believer based on things such as what to eat or drink, and that one should only worship on a particular day, etc. This is reminiscent of some sectarian believers who do not eat pork, or only worship on the Sabbath and judge others who do not do so! This is wrong. If they chose not to eat pork or worship on Saturdays, that is their choice and they should not force what they believe on others.

Yet another characteristic is false humility, and still another characteristic of false teachers is that they go into details with visions and things they have seen and experienced. Another sign of the false prophets and teachers is angel worshiping. They value the angels more than they value Christ. These points are given to you so you may test false teachers and distinguish them from the true ones!

Christian Living

In Colossians 3 and 4 the apostle deals with the ethics and values of Christian living, and he says: *"Therefore, as God's chosen people, holy and dearly loved, clothe yourselves with compassion, kindness, humility, gentleness and patience. Bear with each other and forgive whatever grievances you may have against one another. Forgive as the Lord forgave you. And over all these virtues put on love, which binds them all together in perfect unity. Let the peace of Christ rule in your hearts, since as members of one body you were called to peace. And be thankful. Let the word of Christ dwell in you richly as you teach and admonish one another with all wisdom, and as you sing psalms, hymns and spiritual songs with gratitude in your hearts to God. And whatever you do, whether in word or deed, do it all in the name of the Lord Jesus, giving thanks to God the Father through him"* (Colossians 3:12–17).

At the end of the book, Paul pleads to the wives to submit to their husbands and in the same way to husbands to love their wives and not be harsh on them. He also urges children to obey their parents, for this will please the Lord. He also advises the slaves, in those days workers, to obey their earthly masters and they, in turn, must treat their workers well: *"Slaves obey your earthly masters in everything; and do it, not only when their eye is on you and to win their favor, but with sincerity of heart and reverence for the Lord. Whatever you do, work at it with all your heart, as working for the Lord, not for men, since you know that you will receive an inheritance from the Lord as a reward. It is the Lord Christ you are serving. Anyone who does wrong will be repaid for his wrong, and there is no favoritism"* (Colossians 3:22–23). Truly these should be the standards of Christian living. An employee should work as if it is done for the Lord, and an employer must treat the worker with justice and blessings. This is the base of a healthy business and society!

Questions

1. Describe the characteristics of the false teachers.
2. What does this mean: "Christ is the image of the invisible God"?

Memorize

Colossians 3:17

"And whatever you do, whether in word or deed, do it all in the name of the Lord Jesus, giving thanks to God the Father through him."

LESSON 11

I & II THESSALONIANS: *PAUL ON THE LORD'S COMING*

Lesson 11

I & II Thessalonians: *Paul on the Lord's Coming*

INTRODUCTION TO THESSALONIANS

Thessaloniki, **Thessalonica,** or **Salonica** is the second-largest city in Greece and the capital of the Greek region of Macedonia. It is also the capital of the Thessaloniki prefecture. Paul visited Thessalonica, an important commercial city situated on the commercial route. Acts 17:1–9 describes Paul's visit to this city. As Paul and Silas entered this city he visited the synagogue on the Sabbath and began to preach the Gospel to the Jews. Some Jews believed, however, more than the Jews, it was the Greeks who were interested in the Gospel. They believed in Christ and this new faith. Many prominent people among the women also embraced the Gospel. This caused great jealousy among the Jewish fanatics and Jewish leaders. Paul and Silas were chased out of the city, but their teachings and legacy gave birth to a strong Church in Thessalonica. This was also the start of severe persecution of the new converts by the Jews and other unbelieving Gentiles.

Therefore, the Thessalonians were well known as the persecuted and suffering Church, and their testimony became an example to many other believers in the region and throughout the world. Similarly, today there are persecuted churches around the world. They are in the Middle East, in some countries in Africa, in China, and in North Korea. Believers are being tortured and persecuted because of Christ, and we should remember and pray for them. We should come out of our comfort zones and do something for them.

TODAY'S JOURNEY

I Thessalonians

This book is Paul's first letter to the Thessalonians and at the same time it is also Paul's earliest letter of all. In this book, Paul praises the endurance of the believers and mentions his longing to meet them since his stay there was short. His teachings emphasize more on Christian living and how the believers should live to please God.

Pleasing God

In Chapter four Paul urges the believers to please God. But what is pleasing God? *"Finally, brothers, we instructed you how to live in order to please God, as in fact you are living. Now we ask you and urge you in the Lord Jesus to do this more and more"* (1 Thessalonians 4:1). Then he urges them to avoid sexual immorality, and to control their bodies. When Paul spoke about controlling one's body, he referred to the body as the spouse's. Since marriage makes the two become one body, he considered man ought to treat his wife as he treats his own body, in a respectful and honoring way! He urges the believers to live a holy life; this pleases God!

Next, Paul emphasizes practicing brotherly love, living a peaceful and quiet life, and not minding the business of others; at the end, he urges each man to earn by working. Every person should work and enjoy the fruits of their labor. That is why if a person can work, it is biblically required for that person to do so and rather than receive social security support from the government. Social security support creates societies where people do not want to work and yet receive wages and money. Monetary support should go to those who are ill, widows, orphans, and those who cannot defend themselves.

Coming of the Lord

The book of Thessalonians is well known for its scripture on the Lord's return. Basically, Paul encourages the believers in this city to meditate and hope for the Lord's coming. He did that because he knew the Thessalonians were suffering and being persecuted. He mentions how Christ will return and how those who persecuted them will be punished and cast out of the Lord's presence. Then in 1 Thessalonians 4 Paul explains how the Lord will return from heaven with a loud command and with the voice of an archangel and a trumpet call of God. The dead in Christ will rise first, and then those who are alive at that time will be caught up together in heaven and we will live forever with him (1 Thessalonians 4:16–18). In Matthew 24, Jesus Christ Himself explains about the end time.

II Thessalonians

In reaction to Paul's teaching in I Thessalonians, some false apostles and teachers infiltrated among the believers and began to teach that the Lord's Day had already taken place. Some of the believers were discouraged because they thought the Lord has already returned and they were left alone. Some misinterpreted the teachings of Paul and began to live an ungodly life because they thought everything has already ended. They thought that Jesus did not save them, therefore they lost hope. In connection to this, Paul wrote II Thessalonians to instruct the believers and give them the hope that Christ has yet to return. He also warned against the idleness caused by the wrong teachings of the false apostles.

Eschatology

Eschatology is defined as the body of religious doctrines concerning the human soul in its relation to death, judgment, heaven, and hell. Basically, eschatology means the study of the end times and everything connected to that. There are many disagreements about the signs and the way Christ is going to return, but one thing is sure: He shall return. This should not make us lazy and visionless. Some people live like this because they think that everything will come to an end anyway and then we will be in paradise with Christ and have an eternal vacation. This is wrong! We as Christians should hope in Christ's coming, but we also have to prepare the Church and the world for this coming! Therefore, as believers, we have to be the best in everything; the best parents, best in schools, universities, politics, economy, art, music science, and many other aspects of society, so that we can be the salt of the world and transform our societies for the sake of Christ.

Questions

1. What are the elements of pleasing God?
2. Read entire Matthew 24, and write the points you believe will take place before Christ comes back.

Memorize

2 Thessalonians 5:19

"Be joyful always, pray continually; give thanks in all circumstances for this is God's will for you in Christ Jesus."

LESSON 12

I & II TIMOTHY: *PASTORAL EPISTLES PART I*

Lesson 12

I & II Timothy: *Pastoral Epistles Part I*

INTRODUCTION TO TIMOTHY

First and Second Timothy, along with the book of Titus, are called the Pastoral Epistles. From these three letters, two are for Timothy and one is for Titus. Both are Paul's spiritual sons. He wrote them these letters as a form of instruction about Church governance and leadership. Often, those who have the administration of churches use these letters; however, these letters are also full of wisdom and instructions for Christian living.

Who was Timothy? Timothy was first mentioned in Acts 16. He lived in the area of Derbe and Lystra, where Paul had made many disciples on his first missionary journey (Acts 14:6–22). His father was Greek but his mother, Eunice, was a Jewish believer. His grandmother, Lois, was also a believer (2 Tim. 1:5). Timothy was already a believer at this time; the brothers at Lystra and Iconium spoke well of him (Acts 16:2). It could be that Paul led him to faith in Christ on his first missionary journey. It could also be that his mother and grandmother were the instruments of his salvation (2 Tim. 1:5). The Scripture is silent on the specifics of Timothy's conversion; nevertheless, Paul considered himself the "spiritual father" of Timothy, calling him "a true son in the faith" (1 Tim. 1:2).

Timothy was one of the favorite companions of Paul on his mission trips. Later, Paul sent him to Ephesus as an overseer and leader of that church.

TODAY'S JOURNEY

I Timothy

The theme of this letter is the right behavior in the household of God. Each chapter speaks to a theme concerning that behavior:

- Chapter 1 speaks of sound doctrines and false teachings
- Chapter 2 speaks on prayer and worship
- Chapter 3 speaks on the matter of church leadership
- Chapter 4 speaks on apostasy (abandonment of religious or political beliefs)
- Chapters 5 & 6 speak on pastoral administration

Sound Doctrines & False Teachers

In Chapter 1, Paul re-tackles the issue of false teachers, and states that Timothy should hold to sound doctrines. He gave the authority to Timothy to command false teachers not to teach wrong doctrines. He describes to them how they should teach: *"So that you may command certain men not to teach false doctrines any longer nor devote themselves to myths and endless genealogies. These promote controversies rather than God's work-which is by faith. The goal of this command is love, which comes from a pure heart and good conscience and sincere faith. Some have wandered away from these and turned to meaningless talk"* (1 Timothy 1:3–6).

- They devote to myths
- They devote to endless genealogies
- They promote controversies

They like to speak about myths and spooky mysteries about God; their teachings are more on the supernatural and controversial experiences. Paul emphasizes God's work in faith and love from a pure heart. At the end of the story, the false teachers have all the right things and even supernatural performances, but not love for God or for others. Love is the sign of a true teacher. Love does not mean agreeing with the evil in a person or accepting everything: Love means telling the truth even if it hurts — love which comes from a pure heart.

Orderly prayer and worship

- Pray for the authorities (1 Timothy 2:1)
- Lift up hands in prayer without anger (1 Timothy 2:8)
- Woman should be quiet and dress modestly (1 Timothy 2:9–15)

In 1 Timothy 2, Paul first urges the Church to pray and intercede for kings and government leaders so believers can live in peace. This should be the attitude of the Church today; we have to pray for our kings, presidents, leaders and governors. Regardless of who they are, we have to pray for them. This stimulates social transformation. Then he instructs the Church to pray with open hands, open hearts, and without anger or disputing. Sometimes church members have problems with each other, and yet they come and pray; this is not acceptable to God.

Next comes the most controversial issue: Paul's teachings on issues about women. He says that women should dress modestly and gently, and their beauty should be based on their deeds rather than their appearance. Then he urges women to be quiet and not teach in the church. There are many controversial teachings on this subject. Some religions in the Christian faith allow women to teach and preach, while others refuse.

Speaking of Local Church Leadership

Overseers or Bishops

Speaking of Leadership for the local church, Paul also gave some instructions to the leaders, overseers, and deacons. In 1 Timothy 3:1–7 Paul gives some characteristics of true Overseers or Bishops:

- Above reproach
- The husband of one wife
- Temperate
- Self-controlled
- Respectable
- Hospitable
- Able to teach
- Not given to drunkenness
- Not violent but gentle
- Not quarrelsome
- Not a lover of money
- He should manage his house first
- He must not be a recent convert
- He must have a good reputation
- His children should obey him

Deacons

In 1 Timothy 8–13 Paul describes the deacons:

- Men worthy of respect
- Sincere
- Drinks not too much wine
- Not pursuing dishonest gain
- Holding on the truth of faith
- With a clear conscience

- They must be first tested, then let them serve as deacons
- Their wives should be women of respect
- Not malicious talkers
- Temperate and trustworthy
- Husband of one wife
- Manage his own children
- Those who have served well and stand excellent in their faith

All these characteristics are given to us so that we can know the truth, and follow leaders who are taking these characteristics as their tool for leadership and life.

Speaking of Apostasy

In the last days Paul spoke that many will abandon their faith by listening to deceiving spirits and things taught by demons. These teachings come through hypocritical liars; they impose harsh teachings, forbid people to marry, and order them not to eat certain food (1 Timothy 4:1–5). We can see today some of these points, even in Christian groups where priests are not allowed to marry, etc.

Paul urges Timothy to teach these things, and asks him not to let anyone look down at him because he is young. He also reminds Timothy not to forget the gift he has received through the prophetic message of laying of hands. Every leader should remember his gifts and the day hands were laid on him to do the work of God.

Speaking of Pastoral Oversight

First of all, Paul gave general instructions to Timothy:

- Do not treat an old person harshly, but do as if that person is your father or mother

- Treat younger ones as your brother/sister
- Give recognition to widows in need, and let their children help them
- No one should be put in the list of widow, unless she is above 60 years old.
- Teach the younger widows either to marry or work, otherwise they become idle and go from house to house for help and promote gossip
- Teach everyone to provide for his immediate family, otherwise they have denied their faith.

Some Church Governance Issues:

- An elder, a leader who works hard in preaching and teaching, needs a double honor.
- Do not entertain an accusation against an elder unless it is done by two witnesses
- Do not hurry to lay hands on someone — meaning do not give away position so quickly or do appoint leaders so rapidly.

II Timothy

II Timothy was the last letter Paul wrote. This was written some time after he wrote I Timothy. He was a prisoner in Rome's dungeon expecting to be executed (2 Timothy 4:6). In this letter, Paul speaks of his life as a soldier of Christ (2 Timothy 2:3). He urges Timothy to imitate him. Courage and steadfastness were Paul's characteristics. In this letter, Paul is concerned about those who fall away from their faith.

He also speaks of the last days and that people will be lovers of money. This book can be likened to an instruction book from a father who is about to die and pours out himself into the life of his son.

Questions

1. What are the characteristics of a true overseer?
2. What does Paul teach about money in the book of I Timothy?

Memorize

2 Timothy 4:7

"*I have fought a good fight, I have finished the race, I have kept the faith. Now there is in store for me the crown of righteousness, which the Lord, the righteous Judge, will award to me on that day...*"

LESSON 13

TITUS: *PASTORAL EPISTLES PART II*

Lesson 13

TITUS: *PASTORAL EPISTLES PART II*

INTRODUCTION TO TITUS

Titus looks much like 1 Timothy and was written at the same time. Titus was one of the disciples of Paul. Paul trained him to pass on his teachings to others and to the next generation. Just like Timothy, he traveled with Paul. Titus was a gentile convert. Titus traveled with Paul to Crete, an Island in Greece and was commissioned by Paul to stay there and teach others. In this letter, Paul instructs Titus on organizational matters of the local church. Here are some directions concerning:

TODAY'S JOURNEY

Elders (Presbuteroi)

Paul urged Titus to appoint elders in every city on the island to teach and instruct churches. He basically speaks of the same things he mentioned in I Timothy. Elders should be blameless and the husband of one wife. Their children should be believers, and there are many other characteristics which are found in Titus 1: 5–9.

False Teachers

Paul mentions a group called the "circumcision group" (1:10). This group strongly proclaims Jewish traditions to Christianity. Paul advises Titus to rebuke these people sharply so that they will be sound in their faith and will pay no attention to Jewish myths or to the commands of those who reject the truth (Titus 1:13–14). This group was too much in the "clean and unclean aware" sort of faith, living in the bondage of the Law. Paul said: *"To the pure all things are pure, but to those who are corrupted and do not believe, nothing is pure. In fact, both their minds and consciences are corrupted"* (Titus 1:15).

Sometimes the body of Christ needs a sharp rebuke. Only then we can wake up from our deep slumber. When we ourselves are impure, we look at things rather impurely. Life is a matter of how we look at things. Christianity should also be this way. We are now free from all kinds of Jewish myths and by-laws because we are saved by grace. Nothing is unclean to touch and to eat if we believe so.

Do Not Quarrel

Paul also warned Titus (and he is still warning us) not to enter into discussions and arguments about the Law because they are unprofitable and useless. He mentions that those who do so divide the Church, so it is better to have nothing to do with them after warning them (Titus 3:9–11).

Other Matters

Paul also requests that Titus teach older men to act as mature men and older women to live a life of dignity, young men to be self-controlled, and slaves to obey their masters, so that the Gospel is well represented to the unbelievers (Titus 2).

Conclusion of the Matter

Paul's closing remarks are that Christians should learn to devote themselves to doing what is good, that they may provide for daily necessities and not to live unproductive lives (Titus 3:14).

Questions

1. What are the characteristics of an elderly man / woman in the Lord?
2. What was the circumcision Group?

Memorize

Titus 1:15

"To the pure all things are pure, but to those who are corrupted and do not believe, nothing is pure. In fact, both their minds and consciences are corrupted."

LESSON 14

PHILEMON: *A FREE SLAVE*

Lesson 14

PHILEMON: *A FREE SLAVE*

INTRODUCTION TO PHILEMON

This is a letter with three main characters: Paul, Onesimus, and Philemon. Onesimus is a slave in Colosse who has robbed his master Philemon and ran away. On his flight, Onesimus met Paul in Rome, came to Christ, and became a devoted Christian. Paul was in prison when he was writing this letter.

TODAY'S JOURNEY

Paul understood the Christian duty of the slave (worker) to his master (employer) and therefore with a letter written to Philemon, he sent Onesimus back to him. The master Philemon was a devoted Christian, and therefore Paul knew that he would understand Onesimus' condition and forgive him. Even though the size of this letter is marginal, the interpretation can contain the pages of a book on its own. There are certain things that need to be discussed.

First of all, the slave/master topic in the New Testament should be seen as an employee-employer relationship. This has little to do with the definition of slave definition as we have known it since the 15th or 16th century. The misinterpretation of the word "slave" has lead the Church to do cruel things in the name of Jesus, which brings us to the second point: we are all aware that slavery is a shameful stain in the history of civilization, especially in the western civilization. In the name of Christ and the Church, the western world enslaved others and colonized nations of which the results are still obvious. There were times in history when slavery was tolerated and even justified through Christian faith. However, this little book in the New Testament is proof that slavery is not tolerated by Christ and does not fit in the doctrine of Christian faith. In fact, we read that Philemon is about a liberated slave, Onesimus, who was freed from injustices done to him, and at the same time is the story of a liberated slave master, Philemon, who was freed from wickedness of his own actions. Onesimus was enslaved by the slave master, and Philemon, the slave master himself, was enslaved by the cruelty and evil of his own heart! However, now the slave master and the slave are brothers through the saving gospel of Jesus Christ.

One African Christian told me that even today some people in Africa think that God is white. *"When the white men came to Africa and taught us the Gospel, they always painted Jesus as a white man and they taught us that He is God. So If God is white what am I suppose to be as a black man? The devil?"* he said.

Total Transformation

In the beginning of this lesson, I mentioned that Onesimus was a slave who robbed his master and fled. Many people look at this superficially. Why did Onesimus rob his master? Can it be because Onesimus was treated unjustly, incorrectly, rudely, and poorly paid for his wages? Every reaction is the result of an action; perhaps Onesimus was so badly treated that he was capable of robbing his master and running away until he met Paul and heard the gospel, which lead him to become a transformed man. The Gospel of Jesus Christ can change the whole identity of a man. This does not justify what Onesimus did, but it helps us see that to answer evil with evil makes the world to become doubly evil. Paul, in his letter to Philemon, mentions that Onesimus was formerly useless but now he is changed: he is a brother, a beloved son, a co-worker, and believer in the Lord. This is what the Gospel can do when it is properly received with an open heart! Still today God changes people. The Holy Spirit can convict us of sin and help us to change. In Christ the old things are gone, the new things have come: only Christ can make us new!

Questions

1. Try to read the book of Philemon carefully and make a one-page essay concerning the life and circumstances of Onesimus and his relationship with Philemon, his master.
2. What is your analysis of the events that took place, and finally what lessons can the reader learn from Paul's words?

Memorize

Philemon verse 11
"Formerly he was useless to you, but now he has become useful both to you and to me."

LESSON 15

CLOSING REMARKS: *LAST JOURNEY*

Lesson 15

CLOSING REMARKS: *LAST JOURNEY*

The Apostle Paul's life was indeed a journey of hope, faith and love; a journey of reformation. Paul's life was a journey from a persecutor of Christ into Martyr for Christ. The process of Paul's ministry shows a very humble ending, which should be taken as an example to all of us; in the beginning of his ministry Paul often addressed himself as an apostle of Christ; gradually he saw himself as a servant of Christ. The humbling process continued in his life, and we see Paul calling himself slave of Christ and prisoner of Christ; near the end of his life, he even called himself the head of the sinners, while at the end we call him a martyr for Christ.

Paul knew much, yet considered himself to know nothing. He began to understand that as he grew in faith and in age, his knowledge was not sufficient, that there were many things he had yet to know and discover for Christ, yet he kept on running the race, winning every battle in the name of Jesus. I hope every Christian begins to realize that our knowledge is limited, and out of this limitation we share our knowledge. This should make us humble and hungry for the will of God in our lives. This should help us to realize that we are no better than others, and that we too are full of mistakes and shortcomings. It is the grace of God who gives us access to appear before the Lord wholly and blameless.

Lastly, we must learn like Paul did to fight for justice, love, and the righteousness of God. We should love all people unconditionally as Christ demanded us to do and as Paul encouraged us to do. In our world today there are many injustices done to the poor, the oppressed, to those who have different beliefs or religion than us, and those on the margins of society. We need to practice unconditional love. I hope this book challenges you to do so. If you have testimonies to share or letters to write, do not hesitate to write me. Thank you for reading this book, and until next journey, remain blessed!

Samuel Lee

ABOUT THE AUTHOR

Samuel Lee graduated from Leiden University with a degree in Sociology of Non-Western Societies. He also has a PhD in Sociology and a Habilitation from the University of Herisau. He specializes in cultural and religious sociology in Japan. His four years of habilitation research resulted in the book *Rediscovering Japan, Reintroducing Christendom: 2000 Years of Christian History in Japan* (University Press of America: Hamilton Books, 2010).

Samuel Lee is the founder and president of Jesus Christ Foundation Ministries and Samuel Lee World Evangelism, which reaches nations with the gospel of Jesus Christ. He has established churches and ministries in Cyprus, Ghana, Nigeria, and the Philippines. Samuel Lee World Evangelism offers tapes/videos/CDs and DVDs free of charge to all who reside in developing or underdeveloped nations. From prison cells in South Africa to schools in Ghana or churches in Japan, Korea, and the Philippines, Samuel Lee's ministry reaches more than 80 nations worldwide.

He is also the founder and president of Foundation University: Education Without Borders, which offers tuition-free academic/theological education for less-privileged migrants and citizens of the developing world. Foundation University is a private non-governmental institution and a member of the European Evangelical Accreditation Association.

Samuel Lee has worked to create and support programs for the rights of undocumented migrants in the Netherlands, and he has helped to establish organizations defending the rights of these migrants. He also won an African Roots Movement award in 2008 for his solidarity with the African community in Amsterdam.

He has often been a guest on television programs for *Family7*, a Dutch Christian Channel, as well as on the *Sid Roth Show* in the USA. He has been featured in various Christian newspapers in the Netherlands, such as *Nederlandse Dagblad* (October 6, 2007).

In November 2004, he was featured on the cover of *Ministries Today*, a magazine for Christian leaders in the USA.

He is the author of several books with the latest being released in early 2010, *Rediscovering Japan, Reintroducing Christendom: 2000 Years of Christian History in Japan* (University Press of America: Hamilton Books), and in February 2008, *Understanding Japan Through the Eyes of Christian Faith* (iUniverse). His other recent titles include the following: *Journey with Paul: A Simplified Survey of the Pauline Books* (Foundation University Press), *Father — a Love Story Untold* (Xulon Press), *Blessed Migrants: A Biblical Perspective on Migration & What Every Migrant Needs to Know* (Foundation University Press). His autobiography is titled *Soldier of the Cross: The Amazing Story of a Muslim who met Christ* (Creation House).

Further, Samuel Lee with his book *Understanding Japan through the Eyes of Christian Faith* has helped train and inspire hundreds of missionaries to reach the Japanese people with the gospel of Jesus Christ.

He is a member of various Christian and scientific associations, such as the Association of Christian Sociologist, the Japan Sociological Society (University of Tokyo), the European Evangelical Accreditation Association, the Japan Evangelical Missionary Association, and many other institutions.

Samuel Lee and his wife Sarah live in Amsterdam and have three children.

About JCF Ministries

Jesus Christ Foundation Ministries is the group name for all the ministries and services offered by Dr. Samuel Lee. Jesus Christ Foundation Ministries consists of the following organizations:

☦ Jesus Christ Foundation Churches

☦ Jesus Christ Foundation Child Aid

☦ Samuel Lee World Evangelism

☦ Foundation University

☦ Foundation University Press

Dr. Samuel Lee's Websites

✞ www.jcfchurch.com

✞ www.slwe.net

✞ www.foundationuniversity.com

✞ www.blessedmigrants.org

✞ www.projectjapan.org

✞ www.samlee.org (Personal Blog)

INVITE DR. SAMUEL LEE

To invite Samuel Lee to speak, please contact info@slwe.net. Samuel Lee is available to give conferences or seminars on the following subjects:

- ✠ **Blessed Migrants Seminar** describes the role of migrants both in the Bible as well as in the current global context.
- ✠ **Anointed For Calling: Discover Your Calling & Transform the World** deals with questions such as "What is my calling?" and "For what has God anointed me in life?" Remember, there is no unemployment in the Kingdom of God!
- ✠ **Touch Me Not Satan** is a challenging seminar on spiritual warfare and the strategy for having a life full of victories. Various spiritual factors are discussed in this seminar, helping us to live our lives on the offensive frontlines.
- ✠ **Understanding Japan** is designed for those who are interested in Japan and have the vision to share the gospel with the Japanese people. Samuel Lee systematically explores various aspects of Japanese culture, society, and Church/Missiological history.
- ✠ **Journey throughout the Old Testament** is a one-week to ten-day seminar dealing with very important basics of the Old Testament.
- ✠ **Apostle Paul** is a one-week seminar dealing with very important aspects of the theology of the Apostle Paul.

✠ ***Church, Poverty, & Social Transformation*** is a two-day seminar on the role of the Church in society for advancing the Kingdom of God in order to bring forth social transformation in our nations. This seminar is created to encourage unity between various denominations as well as promote the establishment of indigenous Christianity and is specially designed for Christians from the developing world.

OTHER BOOKS BY SAMUEL LEE

- **Blessed Migrants** @14.95 U$/12.95 €

A Biblical Perspective on Migration & What Every Migrant Needs to Know

Also available in Audio Book @24.95 U$/19.95 € MP3 format @12.95 U$/9.95 €

- **Soldier of the Cross** @14.95 U$/12.95 €

The Amazing Story of a Muslim Man Who Met Christ

Also available in other languages: Italian, Korean, Japanese

- **Father, A Love Story Untold** @14.95 U$/12.95 €

The Heart of God the Father will be revealed to you in a special way

Also available in other languages: Korean, Farsi, & Tagalog

- **Anointed for Calling** @14.95 U$/12.95 €

Discover your calling and transform the world

Also available in other languages: French & Korean

- **Understanding Japan Through the Eyes of Christian Faith** @ 16.95 U$/14.95 €

A sociological handbook for every Christian who is interested in reaching the Japanese people with the gospel of Jesus Christ

- **Journey with Paul** @ 14.95 U$/12.95 €

A Simplified Survey of the Pauline Books

- **Rediscovering Japan, Reintroducing Christendom** @ 29.95 U$/24.95 €

2000 Years of Christian History in Japan

AUDIO SERMONS

CD SERIES

- What Generosity Can Do? *3CD-Box,* 19.95 U$, 14.95 €
- Touch me Not Satan: *7CD-Box, 34.95 U$,* 19.95 €
- When You Go Through Trials: *3CD-Box,* 19.95 U$, 14.95 €
- Kingdom of Heaven: *3CD-Box,* 19.95 U$, 14.95 €
- You and God: *3CD-Box,* 19.95 U$, 14.95 €
- The Power of Vision: *2CD-Box,* 12.95 U$, 9.95 €

CD SINGLE TITLE

- Samuel Lee's testimony — 7.95 U$, 5.95 €
- Expect a Miracle — 7.95 U$, 5.95 €
- Four corners of Faith — 7.95 U$, 5.95 €
- The True Pentecost — 7.95 U$, 5.95 €
- The Heart — 7.95 U$, 5.95 €
- How to Remain in your Calling — 7.95 U$, 5.95 €
- Justice and Grace — 7.95 U$, 5.95 €
- What Hope Can Do? — 7.95 U$, 5.95 €
- What Is So Special about Woman? — 7.95 U$, 5.95 €
- The God Factor — 7.95 U$, 5.95 €
- Manifesto of Grace — 7.95 U$, 5.95 €
- Power of Love — 7.95 U$, 5.95 €

DVD SERIES

- What Generosity Can Do? 3DVD-Box, 38.95 U$, 29.95 €
- Touch Me Not Satan: Spiritual Warfare Series. 7DVD-Box, 90.95 U$, 69.95 €
- Church: 4DVD-Box, 51.95 U$, 39.95 €
- When You Go Through Trials: 3DVD-Box, 38.95 U$, 29.95 €
- I Will Series: The Promises of God throughout the Bible. 3DVD-Box, 38.95 U$. 29.95 €
- I am "The Key to Success and Happiness": 2DVD-Box, 25.95U$, 19.95 €

DVD SINGLE TITLES

- Marriage — 12.95 U$, 9.95 €
- Relationship and Borders — 12.95 U$, 9.95 €
- Character Matters — 12.95 U$, 9.95 €
- Before anything, I am Human being — 12.95 U$, 9.95 €
- Biblical Rights of Migrants — 12.95 U$, 9.95 €

* Transportation Cost will be added to the price of total items order

TO ORDER

Call Us: 0031-20-699 48 97 ~ 0031-20-4167308

Fax Us: 0031-20-4167309

Email Us: info@slwe.net

Visit Us: www.slwe.net

www.ingramcontent.com/pod-product-compliance
Lightning Source LLC
LaVergne TN
LVHW051839080426
835512LV00018B/2973